CULTURE SHOCK!

Portugal

Volker Poelzl

Graphic Arts Center Publishing Company
Portland, Oregon

In the same series

Argentina	*Ecuador*	*Laos*	*South Africa*
Australia	*Egypt*	*Malaysia*	*Spain*
Austria	*Finland*	*Mauritius*	*Sri Lanka*
Belgium	*France*	*Mexico*	*Sweden*
Bolivia	*Germany*	*Morocco*	*Switzerland*
Borneo	*Greece*	*Myanmar*	*Syria*
Brazil	*Hong Kong*	*Nepal*	*Taiwan*
Britain	*Hungary*	*Netherlands*	*Thailand*
California	*India*	*New Zealand*	*Turkey*
Canada	*Indonesia*	*Norway*	*UAE*
Chile	*Iran*	*Pakistan*	*Ukraine*
China	*Ireland*	*Philippines*	*USA*
Costa Rica	*Israel*	*Portugal*	*USA—The South*
Cuba	*Italy*	*Saudi Arabia*	*Venezuela*
Czech Republic	*Japan*	*Scotland*	*Vietnam*
Denmark	*Korea*	*Singapore*	

Barcelona At Your Door	*Paris At Your Door*	*A Student's Guide*
Beijing At Your Door	*Rome At Your Door*	*A Traveller's Medical*
Chicago At Your Door	*San Francisco At*	*Guide*
Havana At Your Door	*Your Door*	*A Wife's Guide*
Jakarta At Your Door	*Shanghai At Your Door*	*Living and Working*
Kuala Lumpur, Malaysia	*Tokyo At Your Door*	*Abroad*
At Your Door	*Vancouver At Your Door*	*Personal Protection At*
London At Your Door		*Home & Abroad*
Moscow At Your Door	*A Globe-Trotter's Guide*	*Working Holidays*
Munich At Your Door	*A Parent's Guide*	*Abroad*
New York At Your Door		

Illustrations by TRIGG

Front cover photograph by Lonely Planet Images
Back cover photograph by Volker Poelzl
All inside photographs by Volker Poelzl, except for photograph
on page 265 by Katharina Boettcher

© 2004 Marshall Cavendish International (Asia) Private Limited

This book is published by special
arrangement with Marshall Cavendish International (Asia) Pte Ltd
Times Centre, 1 New Industrial Road, Singapore 536196
International Standard Book Number 1-55868-787-4
Library of Congress Catalog Number 2003-112785
Graphic Arts Center Publishing Company
P.O. Box 10306 • Portland, Oregon 97296-0306 • (503) 226-2402

Printed in Singapore

To Paula, in appreciation
of a long friendship across three continents.

CONTENTS

Preface *vii*

Acknowledgments *viii*

Map *ix*

Introduction *x*

A Look at the Land 1

Geography *1*

Population *2*

Portugal's regions *4*

The natural environment *12*

Climate *15*

Time *16*

Portugal Then and Now 17

Prehistory *17*

Roman conquest *18*

The Gothic invasion *19*

Moorish occupation *19*

Independence and reconquest *20*

Consolidation of the kingdom *21*

The Age of Discovery *21*

Portugal's Golden Age *23*

Portugal under Spanish rule *23*

The restoration of
independence *24*

Disaster and tyranny *24*

Road to constitutional
monarchy *26*

Portugal's African
possessions *27*

The First Republic *27*

Military rule and the *Estado
Novo* *28*

The Revolution of the
Carnations *29*

The new Portugal *30*

The economy *30*

Government and political
system *32*

Portuguese Realities 34

Still the poor house of Europe? *35*

Gender disparities *36*

Race relations *39*

A country of emigrants *40*

Internal migration *41*

Rural ways of life *42*

Urban living *43*

Understanding the Portuguese 45

The ever-present past *45*
Traditions and transitions *46*
Neighbors but poles apart *49*
Family life *51*
Sentiments and perceptions *58*

A Deeply Rooted Faith 65

Catholicisim today *66*
Rituals to live by *67*
Religious practices *70*
The Virgin of Fátima *72*
Catholic celebrations and
   traditions *74*
Other religions *77*
Folk beliefs and
   superstitions *78*

Do as the Portuguese Do 79

Greetings *79*
Forms of address *80*
In conversation *81*
Inviting and being invited *84*
Appearances *88*
Manners and demeanors *91*

A Taste of Portugal 97

The Daily fare *98*
Eating in and out *99*
Sustenance from the sea *101*
Hearty meat dishes *104*
Favourite soups *104*
Other specialties *105*
Pastries *105*
Snacks and appetizers *106*
Alcoholic beverages *108*
Coffee drinks *112*

Folklore and Tradition 113

Handicrafts *114*
Traditional folk music *116*
Fado—tunes from the Portuguese
   soul *117*
Folkloric dances *119*
Festivals, fairs, and pilgrimages
   121

Touched by the Muses 128

Literature *128*
Music *132*
Art and architecture *135*
Azulejos 140
Portuguese cinema *142*

Socializing and Recreation 144

Favorite pastimes *144*
Sports *146*
Socializing in public *149*

Out on the town *151*
The performing arts *154*

Moving to Portugal 156

Before you leave home *156*
Entry requirements *158*
Documentation and other
  formalities *160*

Setting up home *162*
Domestic help *166*
Initial adjustments *166*
Expatriates in Portugal *170*

Daily Life 172

Shopping *172*
Postal service *174*
Telecommunications *175*
Financial matters *178*
The media *181*
Getting around *182*

Driving in Portugal *185*
Law enforcement, crime, and
  safety *187*
Health considerations *188*
Healthcare *190*
Education *193*

Work and Business 195

Working in Portugal *195*
Doing business in Portugal *199*

Business etiquette and style *205*

Overcoming the Language Barrier 210

The language challenge *210*
Introduction to European
  Portuguese *212*

Pronunciation *212*
Everyday Portuguese *217*
Gestures and signs *219*

Cultural Quiz *221*
Do's and Don'ts Appendix *226*
Glossary *228*
Calendar of Festivals *240*

Resource Guide *241*
Further Reading *260*
About the Author *266*
Index *267*

PREFACE

When I first began research on this book, little did I know that I would soon be led astray by Portugal's age-old history full of details, anecdotes, and tales. Experiencing Portugal was like walking through the open pages of a history book, and it took me some time to get past legends, castles, ruins, and cathedrals to arrive in the present and see Portugal the way it is today and not how it was 500 or 800 years ago. I realized that in order to understand Portugal today it was necessary to understand it through its past. This book is the result of my journey of discovery that led me from the heather-clad mountainsides of the north to the small fishing towns of the south, and from Paleolithic rock art in the upper Douro region to the steel and glass architecture of Lisbon's Park of Nations. Researching and writing this book was a little bit like wandering through Lisbon's Alfama district, with its myriad stairways and winding narrow alleys that lead visitors astray. Every courtyard required a visit, every alley wanted to be followed, every stairway needed to be explored, and at every step new discoveries awaited me, from a beautiful flower arrangement on a rusty balcony to a market woman engaging me in a friendly conversation.

During my lengthy explorations and research in Portugal I tried to keep in mind the main question: what information, among all this wealth of details, facts, anecdotes, and experiences, would provide essential insights into Portuguese culture for the readers? I wanted this book to be both informative and entertaining, and above all, I wanted to awake in the reader a little bit of that curiosity about Portugal that guided me on my own discoveries. This book is by no means an attempt to cover every aspect of Portugal. It is merely intended as an introduction to the wealth of Portuguese culture and an invitation for readers to lose themselves a little bit in Portugal's rich art, music, history, stalwart castles, and narrow alleys and come out enriched and transformed.

ACKNOWLEDGMENTS

This book would not have been possible without the generous support of my friends, family, and the many Portuguese who have provided valuable insights, information, and assistance. In Tucson, Arizona, I want to thank Carly and Stu for their hospitality and friendship. Thanks also to the 'Banditos,' Shay and Ben, for the much-needed musical diversion, and to Shellie for her friendship and support while finishing the manuscript.

In Portugal I would like to thank Francisco and his cousin Carla for their companionship and hospitality. Thanks also to the international community in Lisbon, especially Rebeca and Gianluca, who have shared many of their insights and observations with me. Thanks also to Mário and Fernando who have provided valuable information. Special thanks to Marjan who let me use her laptop computer after I spilled water over mine, and to Katharina for her companionship on explorations in Lisbon and beyond, and for her special insights and advice. I would also like to thank my mother for her generosity and company during her visit to Portugal.

I would also like to mention my gratitude to the staff of many tourist information offices and historic sights all over Portugal, who have patiently and diligently answered my many questions. Special thanks go to the staff of the Archeological Park in Vila Nova de Foz Côa, the Museu da Terra de Miranda in Miranda do Douro, the tourist information in Bragança, Jorge at the palace convent in Mafra, the very helpful staff at the Braga tourist office, and the always available staff at the various tourist offices in Lisbon. Thanks also to the staff at the Videoteca, the Fonoteca, as well as the Campo Pequeno, Graça and, Belém public libraries in Lisbon for their helpfulness.

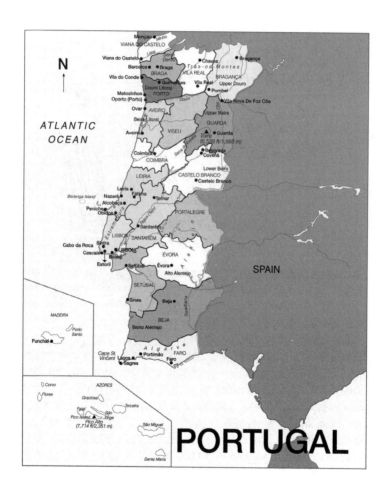

N

ATLANTIC
OCEAN

Monção ● Minho
VIANA DO CASTELO
Viana do Castelo ●
Barcelos ● ● Braga
Vila do Conde ● BRAGA
Guimarães
Douro Litoral
Matozinhos ●
Oporto (Porto) ● PORTO
Ovar ● AVEIRO
Beira Litoral
Aveiro ●
Coimbra ●
COIMBRA
Leiria ●
LEIRIA
Nazaré ● Fátima ●
Alcobaça ●
Peniche ● Tomar ●
Óbidos ●
LISBON SANTARÉM
Cabo da Roca Sintra ●
Cascais ● ● LISBON
Estoril ● Belém ● Setúbal ●
SETÚBAL
Sines ●
MADEIRA
○ Porto
Santo
Funchal ●
Cape St.
Vincent Lagos ●
Sagres ●

Serra do
Gerês
VILA REAL Chaves ●
● Bragança
Trás-os-Montes
Vila Real ● BRAGANÇA
Upper Douro
● Pombal
Vila Nova De Foz Côa ●
Upper Beira
GUARDA
▲ Guarda
Torre
(6,538 ft/1,993 m) ● Belmonte
Covilhã ●
Lower Beira
CASTELO BRANCO
● Castelo Branco
PORTALEGRE
Santarém ●
SANTARÉM
ÉVORA
● Évora
Alto Alentejo
Beja ●
BEJA
Baixo Alentejo
Algarve FARO
● Portimão
Faro ●

Berlenga Island

SPAIN

○ Corvo AZORES
○ Flores
Graciosa ○
Faial ○ São ○ Terceira
Pico Island ▲ Jorge
Pico Alto ○ São Miguel
(7,714 ft/2,351 m)
Santa Maria ○

PORTUGAL

ix

INTRODUCTION

Located on Europe's westernmost perimeter, Portugal leads an almost forgotten existence in the shadow of Western Europe's great nations. Little is known about this small country, except perhaps port wine and the Algarve, Portugal's best-known resort region. Portugal is not a country that readily displays itself or its culture. Portugal does not have world-famous natural wonders and architectural trademarks. Its national heroes are not well-known abroad and there are no long lines outside the Lisbon museums to see the works of Portugal's most famous painters. Portugal is not a country of superlatives or superstars, but it has an enormous cultural and historical depth that goes back several thousand years and gives the country and people their identity. The Portuguese themselves are a humble and somewhat timid people, even a little reserved, and it takes time to get to know them and discover their gentle and benevolent nature. Many people have asked me what it was that I liked best about Portugal, and I have come up with the following answer: "That people still have time, time for friends and family, time to plant kale in their tiny backyards, time to stand under an archway on the town square and just watch the world go by…"

While Portugal has undergone significant changes brought by modernization and its proximity to more progressive nations, it has changed very little in many other ways. Portugal remains somewhat an anachronism among Western European nations. It is a staunchly traditional country, but it is a conservatism that is adaptable and thus able to reconcile the old with the new. Portugal is no doubt changing, but just as in their daily lives, the Portuguese are in no hurry to become modern Europeans. Most Portuguese seem to prefer a healthy balance between old-fashioned ways and new attitudes, and the Portuguese outlook on the future may ultimately be a nostalgic one: one foot rooted in its great past and its beloved traditions, and the other stepping toward a modern future as a well-integrated part of Europe.

The first chapters are intended as an introduction to the country's geography, history, society, and politics, followed by a closer look at Portuguese family life, religion, and customs. The second half of the book deals with Portuguese food, cultural traditions, and the arts, as well as an introduction to living and working in Portugal. An appendix provides a list of useful resources, contacts, and a reading list.

Despite the recent changes, Portugal remains a quiet and unpretentious country whose subtle charm and beauty are not readily and easily discovered, but take time to be appreciated. Only those with a little time to go deeper than a tourist excursion allows will be rewarded with a deeper insight into Portuguese culture and life. This requires some effort, but is most certainly worthwhile. As poet Fernando Pessoa wrote in *Mensagem* (1926):

> "*Valeu a pena? Tudo vale a pena*
> *Se a alma não é pequena.*"
> (Was it worthwhile? Everything is worthwhile,
> If the soul is not small.)

The Douro River, with the city of Porto in the background.

Chapter One

A LOOK AT THE LAND

"*Eis aqui quase cume da cabeça*
De Europa toda, o Reino Lusitano
Onde a terra acaba e o mar começa..."
(Here, almost the tip of the head
Of all Europe, is the Portuguese Kingdom
Where the land ends and the sea begins...)
—Luís Camões, *Os Lusíadas*, Canto III, 20

GEOGRAPHY

Portugal is located on the Iberian Peninsula on the southwestern edge of continental Europe. It is one of Europe's smaller nations with a total land area of 91,951 square km (35,503 square miles), which includes the Azores and Madeira islands. Portugal makes up only one sixth of the Iberian Peninsula, and when looking at a map it becomes obvious that the country only has two neighbors: the Atlantic Ocean and Spain. In fact, Portugal almost seems to be pushed off the edge of Europe by its much larger neighbor. Portugal's coastline extends over 1,793 km (1,114 miles) and the border with Spain is 1,214 km (754 miles) long, a fact that has significantly shaped the country and its people. No matter where you are in Portugal, the Spanish border is never far away, which explains why the inland regions are dotted with castles and fortifications: the border had to be defended against a very powerful neighbor, who in the course of Portugal's long history often turned enemy.

Portugal's topography is best understood when imagining an upright rectangle that is tilted upward to the east and north. The country has a north-south extension of about 580 km (360 miles), and a width varying from 130 to 225 km (80 to 140 miles). Northern Portugal is characterized by high plateaus and mountains. The central region between the Douro and the Tejo is mostly hilly with scattered mountains, wide valleys, and the coastal plain. In the east rise the impressive Serra da Estrela mountains, home to the highest elevation in continental Portugal, the Torre (1,993 m, or 6,538 feet). The land south of the Tejo is generally flat and consists mostly of rolling plains. Several low mountains rise along the Spanish border and also in the northern Algarve.

Portugal is dissected by several large rivers, among them the Minho, Douro, Mondego, Vouga, and Tejo. Most of them have their source in the mountains of western Spain and run west to the sea. All of these rivers are navigable at least for short distances and some of them, such as the Tejo and Douro, were extensively used for transportation in the past.

POPULATION

Portugal has 10.3 million inhabitants. Portugal's population growth rate is small: the population only grew 5% in the past decade. Portugal's population is also increasingly aging. Between 1960 and 2000, the number of elderly people grew by about one million.

A People of Many Origins

The Portuguese population has its origins in several different peoples that settled in Portugal in historic times, such as Celts and Germanic tribes, as well as Mediterranean and North African people. But these ethnic groups have blended together over the centuries, and the Portuguese are today fairly homogeneous. There are more blond and blue-eyed Portuguese in the north due to Celtic and Germanic influence, and more dark skinned and black-haired people in southern Portugal due to the Moorish presence, but these differences are not dominant. Today the Portuguese distinguish each other more through their regional culture and dialect than through actual racial characteristics. Portugal's official language is Portuguese, which is spoken by all citizens.

Urbanization

Until the 1960s, Portugal was largely a rural country. Industrialization and migration from rural areas to cities have since changed Portugal into a more urban society, although Portugal remains a fairly rural country compared to its European neighbors. There are only two large urban areas and a number of small cities. The capital Lisbon has 559,000 inhabitants (1.8 million in the metropolitan area) and Porto has 264,000 inhabitants (1.2 million in the metropolitan area). Other large cities are Braga, Coimbra, Aveiro, Setúbal, and Faro. Sixty-three percent of the population live in urban areas, compared to the average urbanization rate in the European Union (EU) of around 77%.

Immigration

In 2003, there were about 450,000 legal foreign residents in Portugal, a little over 4% of the total population. The total number of illegal immigrants is estimated at about 50,000. Portugal's foreign residents consist of mostly citizens of African descent from the former colonies, Brazilians, Western Europeans, and an increasing number of immigrants from Eastern Europe such as Ukrainians and Romanians. There is also a small minority of Roma (commonly known as gypsies) in Portugal, most of whom arrived here over 500 years ago. There are also more recent arrivals of groups of Romanian gypsies, most of whom are illegal immigrants.

PORTUGAL'S REGIONS

Portugal is divided into several different regions, which do not form political districts but are primarily areas of geographic, historic, and cultural unity. The influence of the natural environment on regional culture is noticeable everywhere, from the granite granaries in the Minho to the schist farm houses in the Beira Alta and adobe cottages still found in the Algarve. In some regions popular festivals follow the growing cycle of grapes; in others they celebrate the wheat harvest, and many towns in the cattle-raising areas hold bullfights as soon as the winter rains end. Regional cuisine relies on locally available ingredients. Goat, hare, partridge, and trout are common dishes in the mountainous regions, whereas Portugal's abundant seafood dominates the cuisine along the coast.

Although the Portuguese are ethnically a fairly uniform people, the different living conditions from north to south have shaped distinct regional mentalities and attitudes. People in the north are traditional and hardworking, and they often subsist on a small, rocky plot of land. They are not nearly as industrious in the south, where the vast plains of Portugal are scorched by the intense sun and few peasants own land. Northern Portugal is also more conservative and Catholic, and it is no coincidence that Portugal's largest sanctuaries, pilgrimages, and religious festivals are all found in central and northern Portugal.

What all of Portugal's regions have in common are the deep historical roots from millennia of human settlement. All across the Portuguese landscape there are stalwart castles built in defense against the Moors, lofty cathedrals erected in the name of faith, and elegant manor houses once home to the rural nobility.

The Portuguese take pride in the unique characteristics of their home region, which are expressed in the livelihoods, crafts, costumes, dances, music, folkloric traditions, dialects, and the very important regional wines. Everywhere in Portugal people love to tell visitors what makes their region special in comparison to others. In Trás-os-Montes for example, a local told me that the Portuguese language was purer and more correct in Bragança than in Lisbon. People from different regions have told me that their wine, food, and desserts were the best the country had to offer.

Minho

The Minho region is named after the river that has its origins in the mountains of neighboring Galicia and forms Portugal's northern border with Spain. It was here that Portugal took shape as an independent nation over 860 years ago. Guimarães still prides itself today in being the kingdom's first capital and the place "where Portugal began." Braga, still Portugal's religious capital, was home to Portugal's first bishops long before the country became a sovereign nation. The Minho was dominated by the Moors only for a short time, and its Christian tradition goes back to the third century A.D., when the diocese of Braga was first established.

Except for a narrow coastal strip, the Minho is a mostly hilly region that rises up to impressive mountain ranges in the northeast, the Serra do Gerês and Serra da Peneda, known as the "Portuguese Switzerland." These imposing mountains are home to Portugal's only national park, the Parque Nacional Peneda-Gerês. Small landholdings, which have been in the hands of the same families for generations, dominate the landscape.

Trás-os-Montes

Trás-os-Montes (which literally means "behind the mountains") is Portugal's most rugged and remote region. Every reasonably level land here is used for small-scale agriculture. The district of Miranda do Douro, found in a remote region along the Douro river near the Spanish border, is home to Portugal's only official minority language known as Mirandês. Mirandês was always considered a local dialect until linguists discovered that it was different enough from Portuguese to be considered a language.

The people of Trás-os-Montes, known as Transmontanos, are staunchly traditional and pride themselves in age-old costumes, festivals, and a hearty local cuisine. Largely unchanged by the progress of the past decades, Trás-os-Montes today lacks infrastructure and employment opportunities to achieve development and growth, so young people move elsewhere to find work. There are many villages with hardly any young people or children, just old people going about their work in the fields as they have done all their lives.

The Douro Region

The Douro region follows the Douro River valley from the Atlantic Ocean to the Spanish border. The Douro is Portugal's second largest river and rises in the mountains of western Spain. Before emptying into the Atlantic Ocean, the river passes through Porto, Portugal's second largest city and an important trade and industrial center. It was this town (known by the Romans as Portus Cale) that gave its name to the medieval county of Portucale and later the kingdom of Portugal. Porto has had a continuous importance throughout the country's history, which has led to a permanent rivalry with Lisbon. Prince Henry the Navigator was born in Porto, and it was from here that the Portuguese naval fleet set out for the conquest of Ceuta in 1415—the beginning of Portugal's maritime exploits. Porto was also home to the first liberal uprising in 1820 and the first republican revolt against the monarchy in 1891.

The upper Douro valley is one of Portugal's most important agricultural regions, thanks to the production of port wine which uses grapes exclusively from this area. Port wine has been the region's most important economic activity, since the English began to import the fortified wine in large quantities in the early 18th century. The upper Douro region is also home to the largest site of Paleolithic outdoor rock art currently known in Europe, scattered along 17 km of the lower Côa River. The archeological findings suggest that prehistoric people lived in the valley during the upper Paleolithic period.

The Beiras Region

The Beiras region extends over all of north-central Portugal from the Atlantic Ocean to the Spanish border and is divided into three zones: the Beira Alta, Beira Baixa, and Beira Litoral.

The central topographic feature of the Beira Alta is the Serra da Estrela, Portugal's largest mountain range and protected area. Since it is the only place in Portugal where snow is a regular, annual occurrence, the Serra da Estrela is the country's only winter ski resort.

Agriculture is hard work in this region. Most of the crops are cultivated on narrow terraces on mountain slopes, where the work is still done by hand. As a result, almost every branch of agriculture depends on subsidies. "There's a subsidy for everything," a local farmer told me. "For planting almond and olive trees, for sheep farms, for the preservation of the old pigeon houses, and even for the breeding of donkeys." The many abandoned terraces, olive groves, and vineyards are evidence of the region's most serious problem: a continuous depopulation as residents seek a better life elsewhere.

The Beira Baixa lies to the south of the Serra da Estrela mountains. Wine is grown here, as well as cereals and produce. Castelo Branco is a center of textile industry.

The Beira Litoral is a relatively low region stretching from the eastern foothills of the Serra da Estrela all the way to the coast. The Dão valley is among Portugal's most famous wine-growing regions.

A view of Lisbon's Alfama district.

The Mondego River, which drains the Beira Litoral, is considered by many to be the most "Portuguese" river, because it is the only major river that originates in Portugal. It passes through the city of Coimbra, one of Europe's oldest university towns, on its way to the sea and has been praised in many of the *fado* (a music genre unique to Portugal) songs of Coimbra's students.

Estremadura and Ribatejo

The region north of Lisbon along the Atlantic coast is known as Estremadura, which includes continental Europe's westernmost point: the awe-inspiring Cabo da Roca, or Cape of the Rock, a land of tall cliffs and a violent sea. The Estremadura coast also includes marvelous beaches, sand dunes, and peaceful fishing villages.

The Ribatejo is a flat and fertile region along the Tejo River northeast of Lisbon. The Tejo (also known as Tagus) is Portugal's largest river. Despite its proximity to the capital, the Ribatejo is still largely a rural area. It is one of the few regions in Portugal where bullfighting is still a passion.

Both Estremadura and Ribatejo have played significant roles in Portugal's history and are in many ways Portugal's heartland. It is home to some of the country's most important historic and architectural sites, such as the Alcobaça monastery, the Batalha Cathedral, the Aljubarrota battle field, and the magnificent convent of the Knights Templar in Tomar.

Lisbon, the capital, is a world in itself. Lisbon stands out as the only large urban area in mainly rural Portugal. It is not only Portugal's largest city, but also its economic and cultural center. Although Lisbon shows some neglect, it is doubtlessly among Europe's most charming capitals with its marvelous setting on seven hills that overlook the Tejo estuary. Lisbon is also home to many of Portugal's important historic monuments.

Alentejo

As the name suggests, Alentejo (*Além Tejo* means "beyond the Tejo") is the region on the far side of the Tejo, and is among the hottest and driest regions in Portugal. The southern or lower Alentejo is Portugal's grain belt and is also home to extensive citrus plantations. Miguel Torga, one of Portugal's most influential 20th century writers and historians, remarked that before entering Alentejo we ought to "break at first our lens of small horizons, and enlarge afterwards the distances by which we normally measure the size of our surroundings." Indeed, the openness of the Alentejo scenery is intimidating. The monotony of the open plains and rolling hills is only interrupted by small whitewashed villages and hilltop castles. The Alentejo has only two rivers of importance: the Sado, and the Guadiana, which is the largest river in southern Portugal and forms the border with Spain as it heads south to sea. The controversial Alqueva dam, which was recently completed, will turn part of the Guadiana River into Europe's largest dammed lake, once it fills up.

Algarve

The Algarve is Portugal's southernmost region with a hot and dry climate. The Serra de Monchique mountain range in the western Algarve is an island of lush green forest in this otherwise dry landscape. It rises 902 m (2,959 feet) and creates a barrier against cooler northern weather, resulting in very mild winter temperatures. The coastal area is divided into the western *Barlavento* (windward coast) and the eastern *Sotavento* (leeward coast). The *Barlavento* region is known for its tall red cliffs, grottos, and idyllic coves, while the *Sotavento* is a flat coast with dunes, sandbars, and extensive estuaries.

The Algarve is the Portuguese region that underwent the longest Moorish occupation. Its Arabic name Al Gharb, meaning "the west" (of the Moorish kingdom of Al Andalus) still testifies to this heritage. Although the tourist invasion of the past decades has had a much stronger impact than the 600 years of Moorish rule, the Algarve today preserves a few scattered remains of its Islamic heritage. The region

The rock formations at the Western Algarve, near Lagos.

also played a key role during the Age of Discovery. It was from the distant outpost of Sagres that Prince Henry the Navigator sent out his expeditions to explore the African coast.

Despite the intense tourism development along the coast there are still several active fishing ports, and the fertile coastal plain is covered with plantations of citrus fruit and almonds. The Algarve is today best known as a beach resort and has become one of Europe's top holiday destinations. Unfortunately, high-rise hotels, recreation complexes, and artificial marinas have all but destroyed the many traditional fishing villages and have turned them into bustling resort towns. Two nature parks near Faro and Sagres protect some of the Algarve's coastal areas, but sprawling development continues at a high pace, and environmental protection is not a priority among local politicians and developers.

The Azores

The Azores archipelago with its nine islands extends over 600 km (373 miles) in the Atlantic ocean, some 1,600 km (994 miles) from Portugal. The Azores were discovered in 1427 at the beginning of the Portuguese maritime explorations and became an important stopover point during later seafaring expeditions. The islands take their origin in volcanic eruptions from the ocean floor that began about 40 million years ago. The cone-shaped volcanic peak Pico on the island of the same name is the highest point on Portuguese territory at 2,351 m (7,713 feet). There are crater lakes, valleys, mountain ranges, plateaus, and a predominantly steep and rocky coastline. Earthquakes are common. Angra do Heroismo on Ilha Terceira, one of the oldest settlements in the Azores, has been declared a World Heritage site.

The Madeira Islands

The Madeira archipelago is located about 1000 km (621 miles) southwest of Lisbon. It consists of two large inhabited islands—Madeira and Porto Santo— and small uninhabited islands of volcanic origin. Madeira is the largest and most populous island and is home to the capital Funchal, the archipelago's largest city. Traditionally an island of fishermen and farmers, tourism accounts today for nearly half of the archipelago's economy, and Funchal has grown into an important vacation resort. Madeira is perhaps best known abroad for its fortified sweet Madeira wine, which is similar to port wine.

THE NATURAL ENVIRONMENT

A Humanized Landscape

Portugal has been settled for millennia, and the landscape has long since been tamed and adapted to human needs. All over the country there is a noticeable human influence on the natural environment that goes back a long time: forests were extensively clear cut to obtain timber for ship building, hillsides were turned into agricultural

terraces, and streams were dammed for mills. However, this transformation has been gentle for the most part. The Portuguese farmers worked the land in harmony with nature and in accordance with what the land could sustain. Due to this long and deliberate transformation of Portugal's landscape, there are today few areas that provide sweeping views of a wild mountain range or valley without recognizable traces of human presence. Sprawling development in recent decades has further reduced the natural habitat of plants and animals. About 130 plant and animal species are endangered, and Portugal ranks first in Europe for the number of threatened species, a fact that clearly hints at seriously flawed environmental protection.

Flora and Fauna

Portugal has a very diverse flora with plants of both Atlantic and Mediterranean origin. The north receives more rainfall and is home to Portugal's largest and densest forests, mostly of pines, firs, several varieties of oak, chestnut, beech, elm, and wild cherry. Valleys and riparian habitats are home to moisture-loving trees such as ash, alder, cottonwood, willow, and plantain. The vegetation of higher altitudes in the mountains to the east and north is adapted to the poor soils of schist. It consists of low shrub forests of juniper, gorse, and cistus, as well as a rich variety of wild flowers and alpine vegetation above tree line. In southern Portugal the dominant vegetation are grasslands and low scrub forests, interspersed with groves of native cork oak, pine, and wild growing fig, almond, carob, and olive trees.

In a small country, where most of the land is cultivated and managed and large reserves are rare, there is unfortunately very little room for wild animals. Most of the large mammals once abundant now only survive in drastically reduced numbers. Portugal's mountainous areas near the Spanish border, such as the Beira Alta and Trás-os-Montes regions, are the last refuge for the few remaining large mammals in Portugal, such as wolves, wild boars, and the Iberian lynx, which only exists in Portugal and Spain. Listed as

The Peneda-Gerês National Park.

endangered 10 years ago, the lynx is now seriously threatened by extinction, mainly due to habitat loss. On the other hand, wild goats, deer, rabbits, hares, foxes, and wild cats are relatively abundant, and Portugal still has a healthy population of otters, extirpated in many other European countries.

Bird life is quite diverse and abundant, since many migratory species pass through annually. Flamingoes, spoonbills, egrets, and herons can be found in the Eastern Algarve and near estuaries, rivers, and the coast in southern Portugal. Storks live in Portugal all year-round and their nests crown light posts and church spires all over southern Portugal. The mountainous areas, mostly in the north, are home to royal eagles, vultures, hawks, owls, and falcons.

There are also numerous reptiles and amphibians in Portugal, among them frogs, toads, salamanders, and snakes (including several poisonous vipers). To get an idea of how abundant Portugal's marine life is, one only needs to go to a fish market, where dozens of different fish, crustaceans, and shellfish are sold. The estuaries are especially rich in marine life, and a walk anywhere along Portugal's magnificent coast reveals a wealth of different shells in all colors and sizes.

Nature Parks

Continental Portugal has 25 major protected nature areas that form part of the Rede Nacional de Áreas Protegidas (RNAP)—the National Network of Protected Areas. This network covers about 6,320 square km (2,440 square miles) of land and includes one national park, numerous natural parks, natural reserves, and protected landscapes. Among the most spectacular mountain parks are doubtlessly the Parque Nacional Peneda-Gerês, as well as the Parque Natural de Montesinho in Trás-os-Montes. Among the most interesting protected coastal areas is the Ria Formosa estuary in the Algarve and the wild and rugged western Algarve and Alentejo coast, known as Parque Natural do Sudoeste Alentejano e Costa Vicentina. The Parque Natural do Douro Internacional is also noteworthy, because it is an effort between Portugal and Spain to protect the magnificent gorge of the upper Douro River.

CLIMATE

Portugal has a mild and temperate climate thanks to its southern location and the proximity to the Atlantic Ocean. However, there are significant regional variances. A maritime climate with wet winters and warm dry summers predominates along the coast and the adjacent plains, while the inland regions have a more continental climate with colder winters and hotter summers.

The interior mountain ranges of Trás-os-Montes and Beira Alta have the coldest winter temperatures in Portugal (lows of around -5°C or 23°F) and usually get some snow. The rest of the country has mild winter temperatures not exceeding 18°C (64°F). Cold spells and snowstorms are rare. The summers are hot and dry inland, especially in the south, where droughts are common. On the coast the summers are tempered by the cool air from the Atlantic Ocean. Depending on local conditions high temperatures in the summer can reach up to 40°C (104°F) on the dry plains of the Alentejo.

Fall usually brings rain in October, although temperatures remain mild. In the beginning of November, there is normally a period of sunshine and warm weather called *verão de São Martinho* (summer of St. Martin) as occurs around the time of that saint's day on November 11. Most of the rainfall in Portugal occurs in the fall and winter, with November and December being the wettest months. The average rainfall in northern Portugal is around 89 cm (35 inches) a year, and the lush Minho region receives as much as 150 cm (59 inches). The rainfall in southern Portugal averages around 51 cm (20 inches).

The climate of the Azores is mild and has little variation throughout the year. It is influenced by the warm currents of the Gulf Stream and the northeasterly winds that bring rainfall year-round. The climate of the Madeira is predominantly subtropical with cooler temperatures at higher elevations.

Over the centuries, the Portuguese have developed their own wisdom about the weather, and there are popular proverbs for just about any weather condition and time of year. Many of them still hold true, such as *"Abril de águas mil"* ("April of thousand waters"), which refers to the usually rainy month of April, or *"Que a chuva e o vento de Novembro não te afastem do teu centro"* ("May the rain and wind in November not throw you off balance"), which aptly describes the challenge of fall weather in much of Portugal.

TIME

Portugal, unlike all other continental European countries, uses the Greenwich Mean Time. This means that Portugal is one hour earlier than central Europe, and five hours later than the east coast of the U.S. Portugal switches to daylight saving time from late March through late October. Madeira is in the same time zone as continental Portugal, but the Azores Islands are one hour behind Greenwich Mean Time, which means that it is one hour earlier than the rest of Portugal.

Chapter Two

PORTUGAL THEN AND NOW

*"Depois da fome, da guerra, da prisão e da tortura
Vi abrir-se a minha terra, como cravo de ternura."*
(After hunger, war, prison, and torture
I saw my country open up like a tender carnation.)
    —from *Portugal Ressuscitado*, lyrics by Ary dos
            Santos, music by Fernando Tordo

PREHISTORY

Although exact dates are uncertain, the presence of hunters and
gatherers in Portugal dates back to at least the upper Paleolithic Age,

anywhere from 30,000 to 20,000 years ago. During the Neolithic Age tribes became more settled and began to engage in agriculture. In the first millennium B.C., Celtic tribes began to migrate across the Pyrenees and settled in fortified villages, known as *castros*, whose ruins can still be found on many hilltops in northern and central Portugal. Over time the local populations merged with the Celtic settlers and absorbed their more advanced culture. During the 3rd century B.C. the Carthaginians expanded their influence from North Africa, and trade was extended to Portugal's coastal settlements.

ROMAN CONQUEST

After defeating Carthage in the Second Punic War (218–201 B.C.), the Roman Empire expanded westward to the Iberian Peninsula. During their conquest the Romans encountered fierce resistance from the local tribes, especially from the belligerent Lusitanians, who lived in today's Beiras region. The region was only pacified in 25 B.C. after a

The largest Roman temple on the Iberian Peninsula is in Évora.

long and drawn-out war. The Iberian Peninsula was incorporated into the Roman Empire and was divided into several provinces. Most of Portugal south of the Douro River became part of the province of Lusitania, which also included parts of western Spain.

THE GOTHIC INVASION

After several centuries of stability and prosperity, during which the Iberian Peninsula was transformed into a cultural and political outpost of the Roman Empire, Germanic tribes invaded the Iberian Peninsula in the early 5th century and effectively ended Roman dominion over the region. To reestablish Roman control, the Germanic Visigoths, an ally and vassal of the Roman Empire, were encouraged by Rome to invade the Iberian Peninsula.

After establishing a kingdom with Toledo in Spain as its capital, the Visigoths ruled the Iberian Peninsula as the heirs of the Roman Empire. They converted to Christianity, began to speak Latin, and used the Roman law and tax system.

MOORISH OCCUPATION

In A.D. 711, an invasion of Muslim Berbers from North Africa brought the Visigothic kingdom to an end, and by 719 almost the entire Iberian Peninsula had fallen into Muslim hands. The Umayyad dynasty ruled the Iberian Peninsula for 300 years, and its capital Córdoba became one of Europe's most splendid and sophisticated cities. The only area of the Iberian Peninsula that remained under Christian control was the kingdom of Astúrias along the Atlantic coast in northern Spain.

In 868, to consolidate and expand Christian rule in the region, the frontier province of Portucale (a name derived from the old Roman port of Portus Cale, the present-day Porto) was created between the Minho and Douro rivers as a buffer zone against the Muslim kingdom to the south. In 1096, the Spanish king Alfonso VI awarded this province to a French count, Henry, in exchange for help in defending the Christian kingdom against the Almoravids, a Muslim sect from

North Africa that had come to dominate the Muslim territories on the Iberian Peninsula during the 11th century.

INDEPENDENCE AND RECONQUEST

It was Count Henry's son, Afonso Henriques (reigned 1139–1185), who achieved Portugal's independence. In 1139, supposedly after defeating a Muslim army in the battle of Ourique, Afonso Henriques began to call himself Afonso I, king of Portugal. In 1143, the Spanish king Alfonso VII acknowledged Portugal's independence. Once firmly established as Portuguese monarch, Afonso I continued his conquests to the south. With the help of English and German crusaders on their way to Palestine, he conquered Lisbon from the Moors in 1147. The final battle of the Portuguese against the Moors took place in 1249 under King Afonso III (1248–1279), when the Algarve was conquered.

The 10th-century castle at Guimarães, Portugal's first capital, where Afonso I was born.

CONSOLIDATION OF THE KINGDOM

The son of Afonso III, King Dinis (reigned 1279–1325), was Portugal's first patron of the arts and of learning, and founded Portugal's first university in 1290. He also encouraged shipbuilding, reforestation and agriculture, which gave him the nickname *rei lavrador* (farmer king). The practice of intermarriage between the royal houses of Portugal and Castile led to Castile's claim to the Portuguese crown when King Fernando's (1367–1383) only heir to the throne, his daughter Beatriz, married the Spanish king Juan I. Concerned about losing their status and privileges under a Spanish king, the Portuguese *Cortes* (an advisory council, or parliament, made up of aristocracy, clergy, and commoners), asked João of Avis, the illegitimate son of former king Pedro I, to assume the Portuguese throne. Juan I, however, insisted on his claim to the Portuguese throne and led a Spanish invasion of Portugal in 1385. The Portuguese forces, outnumbered by a much larger Spanish army, managed to win the decisive Battle of Aljubarrota, with the help of their skillful military leaders and a small force of English archers. After the victory, the Treaty of Windsor in 1386 consolidated the English–Portuguese alliance.

THE AGE OF DISCOVERY

King João's third son, Infante Dom Henrique, better known as Prince Henry the Navigator, became the driving force in Portugal's early seafaring exploits. In 1415, he took part in the conquest of the important trading port of Ceuta in North Africa, which marked the beginning of Portugal's maritime expansion. Around this time the caravel, a fast and modern ship that sailed close to the wind and greatly facilitated Portuguese explorations, made its appearance. In 1419, an expedition sent out by Prince Henry discovered Madeira Island, and in 1427 Portuguese sailors reached the Azores Islands. Skillfully assembled knowledge about navigation and shipbuilding allowed the Portuguese to sail "from their western Portuguese shore, across seas

A sculpture of King Manuel I.

never before navigated," as poet Luís de Camões wrote in the opening verse of his great epic *Os Lusíadas* (The Lusiads).

In 1434, Gil Eanes advanced along the African coast and reached the easternmost point of the African continent, which laid the groundwork for maritime expeditions and discoveries further south. The first African slaves were brought to Portugal in 1443, thus reviving the slave trade in Europe that had been extinct since antiquity.

One of the most notable events of this century of Portuguese discoveries occurred in 1488, when Bartolomeu Dias rounded the Cape of Good Hope. After the discovery of the New World by Columbus in 1492, Spain and Portugal divided the world into two spheres of interest in the Treaty of Tordesillas in 1494. An imaginary line that ran from pole to pole approximately 1,770 km (1,150 miles) west of the Cape Verde Islands declared all newly discovered territories east of the line as belonging to Portugal, while all territories west of this line belonged to Spain.

PORTUGAL'S GOLDEN AGE

Manuel I (1495–1521) the "Fortunate" was the king who most profited from the successful voyages of the Portuguese seafarers. Vasco da Gama reached India in 1498, and Pedro Álvares Cabral discovered Brazil in 1500. To pay a vow after Vasco da Gama's successful return from India, Manuel I built Lisbon's most extravagant monastery, the Mosteiro dos Jerónimos. After Vasco da Gama discovered the sea route to the Far East, it was the appointed viceroys of India, Francisco de Almeida and Afonso de Albuquerque, who consolidated Portugal's monopoly over the maritime trade with the Orient. The Portuguese conquered several cities in Persia and India and established a network of fortified supply and trading posts in Africa, India, and the Far East. In 1511, the Portuguese fleet conquered Malacca, the center of the Malaysian spice trade, and reached the Spice Islands in 1512. In 1557, the Portuguese founded the trading post of Macau on Chinese territory which became Portugal's longest-lasting colony. The territory was only returned to China in 1999.

The many magnificent churches and palaces built during this period of exploration and trade were the most significant symbols of Portugal's newly-found wealth, but the 16th century also gave rise to Portugal's most prolific writers, scientists, and artists, the true mark of a civilization's golden age.

PORTUGAL UNDER SPANISH RULE

Portugal's Golden Age came to an end as quickly as it had begun. Assuming the Portuguese throne at a very young age, King Sebastião (1557–1578) launched a military campaign against Morocco, feeding his obsession with a crusade against the Muslim country. This campaign resulted in the most devastating defeat in Portugal's history. In the battle at Alcázarquivir in 1578, over 8,000 Portuguese, including

King Sebastião and most of Portugal's nobility, lost their lives. Since Sebastião died in battle, his great-uncle, Cardinal Henrique, became king until his death in 1580. Since there was no other legitimate heir, King Felipe II of Spain, a nephew of Portugal's former king João III, invaded Portugal and claimed the throne for himself. This marked the beginning of Spanish rule over Portugal, which lasted from 1580 to 1640. While Felipe II respected Portugal's autonomy and appointed only Portuguese noblemen as royal officials in Portugal, his successors neglected these practices, which increased the resentment of the Portuguese nobility against Spanish rule. Besides, Portugal's resources were increasingly strained to serve Spanish overseas interests and finance Spanish wars.

THE RESTORATION OF INDEPENDENCE

When Spain was weakened from a war with France and a revolt in Catalonia, the Portuguese seized the opportunity to reclaim their independence. The Duke of Bragança was appointed King João IV of Portugal (reigned 1640–1656), but Spain did not recognize Portugal's independence and launched several invasions, which were all defeated by the Portuguese forces. Sixty years under Spanish rule had depleted its finances, and during this period Portugal had also lost its trade monopoly with the Orient. England, France, and the Netherlands now dominated the world's oceans and maritime trade. Portugal needed an economic miracle to help recover its depleted treasury, which occurred with the discovery of gold in Brazil in the 1690s. This sudden tax revenue led to a period of great prosperity. Under the reign of João V (1706–1750), Lisbon became Europe's most splendid capital, and the Portuguese court was the wealthiest in all of Europe.

DISASTER AND TYRANNY

Soon after King José I (1750–1777) ascended the throne, the 1755 Lisbon earthquake put an end to this era of opulence and almost completely destroyed the capital. The earthquake occurred on

November 1, All Saints' Day, during mass, and many people saw the disaster as a punishment from God. Marquês de Pombal, the minister of state appointed by José I, took over the rebuilding of Lisbon and gave the city center a modern grid layout. After the successful handling of Lisbon's reconstruction Pombal took control of politics and virtually ruled Portugal as a tyrant. Pombal was also a fanatical anti-cleric, which resulted in the expulsion of the Jesuit order from all Portuguese territories in 1759. However, Pombal's autocratic rule did not make him many friends, and he was dismissed in 1777, when Maria I (1777–1792), the daughter of José I, assumed the throne.

The Napoleonic Wars

Due to Queen Maria's increasing insanity after the death of her husband and her oldest son, her second son João (later King João VI, 1816–1826) became Portugal's regent in 1792. In 1799, Napoleon came to power and began his military campaign in Europe. He intended to close all ports in continental Europe to British ships and demanded from Portugal to close its ports as well. Since Portugal was a long-time ally of England, it did not comply, and in 1807 Napoleon sent a large army across Spain to invade Portugal. Just before the French reached Lisbon, the Portuguese court fled to Brazil, escorted by an English naval fleet. French and Spanish troops subsequently occupied Portugal, but they were expelled by joint British and Portuguese forces in 1811.

ROAD TO CONSTITUTIONAL MONARCHY

At the end of the Napoleonic Wars in 1814, Portugal saw its territory looted and devastated, while King João VI still remained at his court in Rio de Janeiro. In his absence revolutionary ideas began to take hold in Portugal, and in 1821 a new liberal constitution was drafted that limited the king's powers and privileges. Faced with the increasingly revolutionary situation João VI was forced to return to Portugal. His son and successor to the Portuguese throne, Pedro, remained in Brazil as Prince Regent. Soon after, in 1822, Pedro declared Brazil's independence from Portugal and became Pedro I, emperor of Brazil. After becoming king of Portugal in 1826, Pedro abdicated the throne of Portugal in favor of his young daughter Maria and appointed his brother Miguel as regent. However, the arising power struggle between supporters of constitutional monarchy and absolutism led to a highly unstable political climate in Portugal. With the support of the absolutist faction Miguel appointed himself king, and Pedro saw no other way to help his daughter rightly claim the throne than to return to Portugal and defeat his brother. This led to a civil war (1832–1834), during which Pedro, who favored a constitutional monarchy, was finally able to drive Miguel into exile. Pedro's daughter became queen Maria II (1834–1853), although conflict between the opposing factions of monarchism continued for several more decades.

PORTUGAL'S AFRICAN POSSESSIONS

After Brazil's independence, Portugal's colonial empire was reduced to trading posts in India and the Far East and the somewhat neglected possessions in Africa. When Europe's colonial powers began to divide Africa among themselves in the late 19th century, Portugal took renewed interest in its African colonies. The result was the so-called "rose-colored map," a political plan that established a Portuguese colony across the entire width of Africa, from Angola on the Atlantic to Mozambique on the Indian Ocean. The plan was accepted by Germany and France, but rejected by Great Britain, which intended to control Africa from Egypt south to the Cape of Good Hope. In 1890 Great Britain launched an ultimatum that demanded the withdrawal of Portuguese forces from the disputed territory in Africa or face a war. Intimidated by the ultimatum, the Portuguese king Carlos (1889–1908) withdrew his troops from Central Africa, a decision that was much criticized in Portugal and strongly fueled the republican movement. Still, Portugal was able to hold on to its long-standing claims to Angola, Mozambique, and Guinea.

THE FIRST REPUBLIC

After the humiliating British ultimatum, the movement in favor of a Portuguese republic became immensely popular. The *coup de grace* for the monarchy came in 1908 with the assassination of King Carlos and his eldest son and heir Luís. The king's younger son, Manuel, assumed the throne as Manuel II. His reign lasted less than two years, before a republican uprising by the army and navy put an end to the monarchy in Portugal.

Portugal's first attempt at democratic rule was a difficult and short-lived endeavor. The main agenda of the new government was to reduce the influence of the monarchists and the Church—religious orders were expelled and their property confiscated, and religious instruction at schools was prohibited. During World War I, Portugal

27

sided with its long-time ally Great Britain, and Portuguese troops fought against Germany in Africa as well as in Flanders. Several military coups remained unsuccessful at providing internal stability, and in 1919 a civil war broke out to restore the monarchy, although the republican forces managed to stay in control.

MILITARY RULE AND THE ESTADO NOVO

The instability of Portugal's republican system continued until a successful military coup put an end to the First Republic in 1926. The government that followed was to become Europe's longest dictatorship, which only ended in 1974. To resolve the country's economic problems, military general Carmona appointed economics professor António de Oliveira Salazar as finance minister in 1928. Under Salazar's program of fiscal austerity, Portugal's finances were soon straightened out, leaving room for investments in infrastructure and social services. In 1932, Salazar was nominated prime minister, a post he held until 1968. The new authoritarian political order became known as the *Estado Novo* (New State). Its main allies were large landowners, the commercial elite, industrialists, and the Catholic Church, who all benefited greatly from the new authoritarian government which granted them generous privileges.

During World War II, Portugal remained officially neutral, while secretly supporting the Allies. After the end of World War II, Portugal's main challenge were its overseas possessions. In 1961, Indian troops annexed Goa, Diu, and Daman, the old Portuguese trading ports in India. Starting in the early 1960s, independence movements in Africa began to challenge the Portuguese colonial government. Salazar, however, vowed that Portugal would uphold its overseas empire and defend Christianity and Western civilization, even if it meant that the Portuguese would be *"orgulhosamente sós"* ("proudly alone") in this task. He increased military expenses and sent large numbers of troops to Africa to maintain control of Angola, Mozambique, and Guinea.

THE REVOLUTION OF THE CARNATIONS

When Salazar suffered a stroke in 1968, Marcelo Caetano, a long-time follower, became prime minister. His goal was to carry on Salazar's *Estado Novo* with minor changes, but he had to face an increasingly dissatisfied population and the repercussions of the unpopular war in the African colonies. There was also a growing number of army officers who opposed the colonial wars in Africa and preferred a change of regime. On April 25, 1974, a group of officers who called themselves the *Movimento das Forças Armadas*, or MFA, led a revolt to overthrow the Caetano government. The uprising (which took place during the week that red carnations sprung up in flower shops) originally only included a small segment of the military, but more and more members of the army and navy pledged support for the MFA and the remaining troops loyal to Caetano were unwilling to use force. Under siege by the rebellious army and faced with dwindling support, Caetano abdicated and went into exile.

The MFA quickly appointed General Spínola, an opponent of the colonial war, as interim president to lead the transition to a democratically elected government. A constituent assembly was voted for in general elections in the spring of 1975, and a new constitution was drafted in 1976. The constitution nationalized banking, insurance, transportation, heavy industry, and energy and divided large unproductive estates in southern Portugal into agricultural cooperatives. Soon after the revolution, Portugal began to negotiate terms for the independence of its colonies, which was granted by 1975. As a result of Portugal's withdrawal from Africa, Angola fell into a decade-long civil war, Mozambique was taken over by a Marxist-Leninist government, and East Timor was annexed by Indonesia. In response to the political instability of Portugal's former colonies, over half a million Portuguese settlers fled and returned to Portugal.

With opposing political factions unwilling to compromise, the political climate in Portugal continued to be highly unstable. After a series of minority governments, a coalition government formed by socialist prime minister Mário Soares in 1982 gained enough support to implement important programs and move toward membership in the European Community (EC), which is now known as the European Union (EU).

THE NEW PORTUGAL

In 1986, Portugal became a member of the EC—an important milestone in Portugal's new orientation toward Europe. In the same year, Mário Soares became Portugal's first civilian president since the First Republic. Aníbal Cavaco Silva and his conservative Social Democratic Party governed the country from 1985 to 1995. Under his center-right government, several amendments were made to the constitution. As a result, nationalized industries were again privatized, and the land expropriated under the agrarian reform was returned to its original owners. After a decade of conservative rule, the Socialist Party returned to power with António Guterres as prime minister in 1995 and Jorge Sampaio as president in 1996. After losing in vital regional elections, Guterres called for new general elections in March of 2002. The Social Democratic Party emerged as the winning party, and Prime Minister Durão Barroso formed a coalition government with the small right-wing Partido Popular, the People's Party.

THE ECONOMY

Portugal entered the EC in 1986 as Western Europe's poorest nation. But since then Portugal has made large strides to close this development gap. In the past four decades, the country has changed from a largely agricultural country into a modern diversified economy with a moderately developed industry and a strong service sector. It sustained economic growth of about 4.5% per year from 1986 to 2000. This was achieved largely with the help of substantial structural funds from its European partners. However, its Gross Domestic Product (GDP) per capita is still behind leading EU economies. With the enlargement of the EU in May 2004, much of the aid and foreign investment that have helped Portugal's development will go to the new and poorer member states.

Economic Sectors

The service sector, which includes commerce, transport, communications, tourism, and financial services, is Portugal's most dynamic economic sector. It accounts for 68.9% of the GDP and employs 53% of Portugal's work force. Tourism has become an increasingly important economic sector in Portugal, with about 12 million foreign tourists every year, more than its total resident population.

Agriculture, together with forestry and fishing, accounts for 3.6% of Portugal's GDP and employs 13% of the work force. The most important agricultural products are wheat, corn, potatoes, grapes, wine, olives, wool, meat, dairy products, vegetables, and fruit. Portugal is one of the world's largest producers of olive oil and wine, with port wine as the leading variety. Portugal's agriculture remains in urgent need of reforms and modernization. The productivity is low, and grain and other foods need to be imported.

Although the industrial sector has grown significantly in the past decades, Portugal remains a moderately industrialized country. Portugal's main industrial centers are all located along or near the coast. Heavy industry (steel, petrochemicals, machinery) is localized around Lisbon, Setúbal, and Sines, and light industry (light manufacturing, textiles, shoes) is predominant in Porto, Braga, Aveiro, and several inland cities. The most important industries are still the traditional sectors, such as textiles, shoes, ceramics, canned fish, and paper products. In addition to these main industrial sectors Portugal still has a vital cottage industry based on traditional handicrafts. The most important natural resources are mining (tungsten, iron ore, copper, tin, uranium) and forestry. Cork from Portugal accounts for about 60% of the world's entire production.

31

The Douro region, where the grapes for port wine are grown.

GOVERNMENT AND POLITICAL SYSTEM

Portugal is today a parliamentary democracy. Lisbon is the capital and the country's largest city. Portugal is divided into 18 districts and 2 autonomous provinces. The districts are Aveiro, Beja, Braga, Bragança, Castelo Branco, Coimbra, Evora, Faro, Guarda, Leiria, Lisboa, Portalegre, Porto, Santarém, Setúbal, Viana do Castelo, Vila Real, and Viseu. The islands of the Azores and Madeira are both autonomous regions with a higher degree of self-governance than the districts. Every municipality and parish within a district elects its own representatives and governing body. Portugal's constitution is today firmly based on a capitalistic and democratic society.

Executive Branch

The president of the republic is the chief of state, and the prime minister is the head of the government. The council of ministers, or cabinet, is appointed by the president, following the recommendations of the prime minister. The socialist Jorge Sampaio is the president of the republic until 2006.

Legislative Branch

The legislative branch consists of the unicameral Assembleia da República (Assembly of the Republic), which consists of 230 seats. The members are elected by popular vote in general elections every four years.

Judicial Branch

The Tribunal Constitucional (Constitutional Court) examines the constitutionality of a legislation. The 13 judges are appointed for life by the Assembly of the Republic. The Supremo Tribunal de Justiça (Supreme Court of Justice) is the highest court of law for civil and criminal cases with several subordinate courts. There is also a Supreme Administrative Court, which investigates the administrative conduct of government institutions.

Voting System and Political Parties

All citizens 18 years of age or older are entitled to vote. The president is elected by popular vote for a five-year term. After legislative elections, the president appoints the prime minister, which is the candidate from the party with the most votes.

There are six parties that generally compete for seats in the Assembleia da República. They are the Partido Socialista (Socialist Party), the center-right Partido Social Democrata (Social Democratic Party), the Partido Comunista de Portugal (Communist Party), the right-wing Partido Popular (People's Party), the Bloco de Esquerda (Left Block), and the Partido Ecologista "Os Verdes" (Green Party).

Chapter Three

PORTUGUESE REALITIES

"A Grande e decisive arma é a ignorância. É bom [...] que eles nada saibam, nem ler, nem escrever, nem contrar, nem pensar, que considerem e aceitem que o mundo não pode ser mudado, que este mundo é o único possível."
(The great and decisive arm is ignorance. It is good [...] that they don't know anything, not read, write, count, or think, and that they consider and accept that the world cannot be changed, that this world is the only one possible.)
—José Saramago, *Levantado do Chão*, 1980

Throughout Portugal's history the people have accepted the status quo as a God-given order. Every person had its due place in society and social mobility was not an option or was difficult to achieve. This notion changed little under the anticlerical First Republic and was further expanded under Salazar's dictatorship. The social structure of the *Estado Novo* was based on an elitist and hierarchical division of Portuguese society. A very small and well-established oligarchy ruled the country, while almost three quarters of the population were lower class workers and peasants, who suffered much hardship and poverty. It was not until after the 1974 revolution that major changes began to take place for the majority of the Portuguese population. For the first time the government introduced measures to fight illiteracy and provide health and welfare benefits to the population, as well as raise salaries significantly.

Since the end of the dictatorship Portugal has made significant steps toward becoming a democratic and pluralistic society. As the consolidation of Portugal's democracy went underway, the working class was able to improve its economic situation, and the middle class began to grow and gain influence in society. Upward mobility is now no longer an exception, mostly because of universal access to education. As a result the old class distinctions have become blurred and are no longer as relevant. Portugal's young generation born after the revolution enjoys the most egalitarian conditions that have ever existed in their country.

STILL THE POOR HOUSE OF EUROPE?

Throughout the 20th century Portugal was Western Europe's poorest country. It had the least developed industry, a small service sector, and a backward agriculture based on small farms and large unproductive estates. Even though Portugal's economic growth was among the highest in Europe after joining the EC in 1986, the country is still Western Europe's least developed nation. Undoubtedly, the gap between the EU's wealthier countries and Portugal is narrowing, but the standard of living in Portugal is still far below that of other EU countries. Portugal also has the highest poverty rate in the EU. About

21% of the population live in low-income households, compared to the EU average of 15%. Although nobody in Portugal suffers from hunger, poverty among old people and the rural population is common.

Struggling to Get By

Although Portugal has a social welfare system, the benefits are low and provide minimal financial assistance. The government offers monthly family allowances for children, disability pensions, and social welfare assistance to its needy population, but these subsidies are not enough to get by. Pensions are also low, and workers who have made social security contributions for 30 years could find themselves with a pension of less than 400 euros. As a result of the low pensions, Portugal has the highest percentage in the EU of people of retirement age who still work.

Although the cost of living is lower than in most other EU countries, Portugal has the lowest salary level in the EU. The average annual salary in 2002 was 10,843 euros, compared to 17,600 euros in Spain and 19,000 euros in France. The minimum wage is also the lowest in the EU with 365.60 euros per month. The unemployment rate has also been rising in recent years due to Portugal's economic slowdown, which has affected young people and those in rural areas.

Waiting for Good Luck

Not surprising for a country with the lowest salary levels in the EU, the various weekly lotteries and sports pools are immensely popular. Days before the major lottery drawings city centers and commercial districts all over Portugal are crowded with *cauteleiros* (lottery ticket vendors), often retired or disabled people, who entice the passersby to try their luck at quick fortune.

GENDER DISPARITIES

In Portugal, it is very noticeable that men and women lead different lives with often clearly separated responsibilities and roles, especially among the older generation. While men meet in the town square to chat or play cards, women often stay home to raise the children, prepare meals, and take care of the household. Women are seen sitting outside on the streets, busy with lacework or embroidery, but they obviously do not enjoy leisure activities to the same degree as their husbands do. And when they go out, they are either in the company of other women or accompanied by their husbands. Even when younger women go out at night, they are mostly in the company of other girlfriends. Although Portuguese women today enjoy much more freedom than only a generation ago, they are bound by a stricter behavioral code than men. A man may quickly be forgiven a drunken escapade in a village bar, but a woman would lose her reputation over it.

But since the end of the dictatorship, Portuguese women have begun to move away from their traditional roles. Young women today no longer see family and household as their only responsibilities, and they mostly share the same social spaces as the men their age. For

An afternoon of needlework on a village street.

them the distinct gender segregation that characterizes the generation of their parents and grandparents is no longer a reality. Young women today also enjoy more sexual freedom, and the once-so-important virginity is no longer a decisive factor for marriage. However, some of the traditional values still persist among the rural population and the lower social classes.

The Struggle for Equal Rights

Historically, Portugal's women were mostly confined to the home and had few responsibilities outside the domestic area. It was not until 1976 that the new constitution gave women the same legal rights as men. Women received the unrestricted right to vote at age 18 and were granted equality in marriage. In recent decades, women have inched ahead of men in terms of education. Around 57% of Portugal's university students are women, the highest rate in the EU.

But this advantage in education has not translated into economic equality. Although the law prescribes equal pay for equal work, women on average still earn considerably less than their male counterparts in the same professions. While equal pay has been accomplished to a higher degree in public service, women employed in the private sector are subject to larger inequalities in the pay rate.

Between the Hearth and the Office

Women in Portugal face unprecedented challenges today. On one hand their education qualifies them for leading positions in the economy and public life, but on the other hand traditional views, often held by the women themselves, limit their career choices. Women are still seen and often still see themselves as mainly responsible for the family and the household, which is often in conflict with potential career choices or opportunities that may arise.

A big obstacle to the professional success of Portuguese women is the widespread unwillingness of their spouses or partners to help with domestic chores. The raising of children is still seen by most men as the exclusive responsibility of the mother, and this ingrained attitude is only very gradually changing.

Despite these difficulties, many Portuguese women have managed to reconcile their career interests with their domestic responsibilities. About 60% of Portugal's women are actively employed today, compared to the EU average of 54%. But although there are several female mayors, as well as cabinet ministers in the Portuguese government, the number of women in professions traditionally dominated by men is still small. Portugal had its first female prime minister in Maria de Lourdes Pintasilgo (1979–1980), but this fact has helped little to change the prevalent gender roles in Portugal. In 2003, only 20% of the members of the Portuguese parliament were women.

RACE RELATIONS

It is interesting to note that despite its long involvement in global affairs, Portugal is not a multicultural society, unlike other former European colonial powers. Portugal's colonization has given rise to multicultural conglomerates such as Brazil, but the mother country has never had a large number of immigrants or a multiethnic population.

Most immigrants who live in Portugal today are from former Portuguese colonies in Africa, Asia, and Brazil, or more recently from Eastern Europe. These immigrants are welcome to work in low-paying jobs, but they are otherwise not well integrated in Portuguese society. In fact, there is a noticeable segregation between immigrant ethnic groups and the Portuguese population at large. In Lisbon especially, it is obvious that immigrants keep to themselves in their own neighborhoods and do not easily mingle with the Portuguese. This is related to language and cultural differences and the overall difficulties of adapting to a new country on the part of the immigrants, but it also indicates a lack of interest on the part of the Portuguese. Immigrants not only face a certain degree of cultural prejudice, but also have to confront numerous problems in the work environment, where they are often treated as second-class citizens. They are hired in low-paying positions with minimal benefits, often without a work contract or legal rights, even though they may be legal residents. Although the Portuguese very rarely make explicit racist comments, it becomes obvious upon closer examination that many consider immigrants, especially Africans, as culturally backward and less civilized.

A COUNTRY OF EMIGRANTS

"The Portuguese are found throughout the world—their customs and language span the oceans and cling to many distant lands."
—James M. Anderson, *The History of Portugal*

There are few other countries where emigration has played such an important role in their history and development as in Portugal. Since the majority of Portugal's population have always had a meager existence with limited social mobility, emigration was often the only means to improve their lives.

During the colonial period, the Portuguese emigrated to the trading outposts in the Far East and later to Brazil and Africa. The number of Portuguese leaving their country reached its climax in the 20th century during the *Estado Novo* years. From the late 19th century until the 1960s, an estimated 2.6 million people left Portugal for other countries. Widespread poverty and lack of opportunities under the oppressive Salazar regime encouraged many Portuguese to seek employment abroad. The inheritance system of the small landholdings in northern Portugal also prompted many men to emigrate, since land was often divided into very small plots among descendants, making it increasingly difficult to live off the land. Another significant factor for emigration were the colonial wars in Africa, which required an increasing number of conscripted soldiers in the 1960s. Many young Portuguese men preferred exile to military service in Africa.

Today, close to 1 million Portuguese live outside of Portugal in Europe, and the total number of Portuguese and people with Portuguese ancestry living abroad worldwide is estimated to be at least 4.5 million. Despite large distances most Portuguese emigrants remain closely attached to their home country and maintain their Portuguese cultural traditions. The dream of many emigrants is to earn enough money so they can build a big house and return to Portugal to retire. That this dream has come true for many is recognizable in the very large and somewhat ostentatious vacation homes they build in their native villages, complete with a Mercedes-Benz and swimming pool. Every August, throngs of emigrants return to Portugal to spend their vacation time at home among old friends and family. Many villages hold a *festa dos emigrantes*, a festival in honor of those emigrants who return home for the summer.

Since Portugal has made big strides to modernize and raise its standard of living, fewer and fewer Portuguese seek their fortune abroad or emigrate permanently. But as in the past, rising unemployment and lack of opportunities for young people in rural areas prompt many Portuguese to seek seasonal employment abroad.

INTERNAL MIGRATION

In addition to emigration, internal migration has also had a significant impact on Portuguese society. Starting in the 1940s, when Portugal's industry began to expand, the rural population was attracted by factory jobs in the cities, which prompted rapid growth of urban and suburban areas, a process that still continues today. The sprawling working class suburbs on the outskirts of Lisbon, Porto, and other cities give evidence of how much these urban centers have grown in the past decades. At the same time rural communities, especially in the Upper Alentejo, Trás-os-Montes, and Beiras regions that had been cultivated since ancient times, were suddenly being abandoned. It is not rare to find decaying farmhouses surrounded by abandoned vineyards, olive groves, and almond plantations. Some villages are practically devoid of a young population, but maintain a certain picturesque image as a tourist destination, resembling more an open-air museum than an inhabited place. Many rural communities simply do not have enough economic development or employment opportunities for young people, which is partly the result of a centralized and shortsighted economic policy. Most of the EU development funds of the past decades were funneled into large infrastructure projects that mostly benefited cities and industrial zones. This left much of rural Portugal with an inadequate infrastructure and difficult access to health and social services, education, and jobs. Local administrations in regions most affected by depopulation have developed a variety of strategies to revert this migration trend to the cities. Some towns now pay one-time subsidies for marriages and births, and in other towns childcare facilities and kindergartens are offered free of charge. Whether these initiatives can overcome decades of neglect and prevent further desertion remains to be seen.

RURAL WAYS OF LIFE

Since Portugal really only has two urban areas, small-town life is the most characteristic way of life of the Portuguese people. The pace of life is slow, and it is still the hourly chime of church bells that indicates the passing of time, much more than the nervous pulse of quartz watches. The social network is intimate, and communities are fairly close-knit. In villages, most people know each other by name. People know they can trust each other and they are often more outgoing, hospitable, and friendly than city folk. Businesses are small and family-operated, and children often help their parents in daily activities, be it on a farm or in a small restaurant. Sunday is a day of rest. Most businesses are closed, even bakeries, cafés, and restaurants. Sunday mass unites the majority of inhabitants of small towns and villages and brings all generations together—widows clad in black, elderly couples, as well as young families and children.

URBAN LIVING

Decaying Charm

Portugal's cities are very charming. There are many castles, cathedrals, and historic buildings that create a magical historic atmosphere. But upon closer inspection it becomes obvious that it is really a decaying charm that characterizes most cities. Wherever one looks one sees crumbling facades, roofs covered with plastic tarps, and buildings wrapped in netting and held up by metal scaffolds. Hundreds of buildings in Porto and Lisbon are in urgent need of renovation, and unless this happens soon, most of them will deteriorate beyond repair in a few years. One of the reasons for the neglect of old buildings in city centers is the fact that strict rent control laws make it unattractive for landlords to renovate them. Rapid urban growth has led to the construction of ugly tenements in the suburbs. On the outskirts of the city or in run-down neighborhoods, small clusters of shantytowns, known as *bairros de lata* (tin districts), are common. Here, people live illegally in primitive living conditions, often without electricity, water, or a sewer system. Such slums are often the direct result of the lack of affordable housing in Portugal's cities.

Bringing Green to Urban Gray

One of the most noticeable deficits of Portugal's cities is the lack of green spaces and recreational facilities for their citizens. Playgrounds are also few and far between, which is strange for a country whose people are child-loving. In a country as soccer-crazy as Portugal, it is also surprising to find so few soccer fields in the cities. Children play on squares and even stairways, and make do with whatever small space they can find. I remember observing a group of children playing soccer on a small square in front of a church entrance. When the priest walked by and entered the church, he exchanged a few words with the children, but was otherwise not bothered by their game. At least in

Old buildings line Portugal's narrow alleys.

Portugal's tight urban spaces, people are tolerant of each other and, fortunately, especially of children.

On a positive note, while large green spaces are mostly absent from Portuguese cityscapes, the small squares and parks are always landscaped with much care and devotion and are kept beautiful year-round. That the Portuguese love plants and have a green thumb is also reflected in the tiny balconies that overflow with flowers and houseplants. And wherever there is even a smallest yard, ledge, or terrace, people keep a vegetable patch with kale and other greens, as though the Portuguese need to bring the countryside closer to their urban abodes, as though the vegetable patch with a few sad stalks of kale could satisfy the *saudades*, the longing for the days in the village, that are now long gone.

Chapter Four

UNDERSTANDING THE PORTUGUESE

"O bom Português é várias pessoas."
(The good Portuguese is various persons.)
—Fernando Pessoa

THE EVER-PRESENT PAST

To understand how the Portuguese look at themselves and at the world, it is essential to understand the complex history of this small country. It seems that, more than in any other Western European nation, the strong arm of history reaches to the present and influences people's decisions and thoughts. In Portugal, history is not an abstract field of study that fills libraries that nobody visits. In Portugal history is alive every day of every year. It is alive in the political debates, and in the newspaper editorials. It is alive in how the people live their daily lives, and is reflected in their opinions. Historic events serve as metaphors for the problems and solutions of the present, and to use historical references in conversation seems to be the true mark of an educated person. I was able to experience first-hand this aspect of Portugal's ever-present past. I was at a Christmas concert at the Lisbon Mártires Church, when the local priest addressed the audience with a few opening words. He talked about the fact that this church was among the first to be founded after the conquest of Lisbon in 1147. He then continued to praise the brave Portuguese soldiers who freed Lisbon from the Moors and made it a Christian city. His praise came exactly 855 years after the event, but he spoke with so much conviction and passion, as if the conquest of Lisbon had occurred only a few years back. Apparently the Portuguese did not find it strange to listen to such a passionate speech about an event that took place at the dawn of Portuguese history, since, unlike foreigners like me, they still related to the event just as the priest did.

TRADITIONS AND TRANSITIONS

A scene from Alain Tanner's 1983 movie *In The White City*, although filmed over twenty years ago, is still very symbolic for Portugal. A sailor, who jumped ship in Lisbon, pointed at the clock in his hotel and said to the waitress "Your clock there moves backwards." "No, the clock moves right," she replied. "It's the world that moves backwards." Indeed, the Portuguese have their own clock, a cultural and collective clock that ticks differently from that of other countries, and sometimes even moves backwards. Life in Portugal really does not progress in a linear way or on a time line. It does not move inexorably forward, like a clock. Instead, Portugal seems to move back and forth between the past and the present, between modernity and age-old traditions. Some visitors may call Portugal backward, but it would be more appropriate to describe it as a country that simultaneously belongs to several different ages. Within an hour for example, simply by crossing Lisbon's modern Vasco da Gama Bridge, one can get from the futuristic Portugal of the Parque das Nações (Park of Nations) to a small village in the Alentejo where horse-drawn carts are still in use.

One of the factors that keep Portugal rooted in the past is a strong sense of tradition that pervades all aspects of life. While most Western European countries have renounced traditional ways of life in favor of a modern consumer culture, the Portuguese may have adopted their own solution for the issue of modernity: progress, yes, but not without respect for traditions and for the past. The most visible results of this attitude are the cultural traditions such as folk music, dances, and handicrafts that are still vibrant in every region. The modern urban consumer culture has certainly made its entry into Portugal, but it is not yet a dominant value in Portuguese society. The Portuguese, being poorer than other Western Europeans, still reflect a contentedness with the simple pleasures in life. More than anything else, they treasure social relations based on family life and community.

Wrestling with Change

The Portuguese are strongly patriotic and proud of their culture and traditions, and change is only accepted slowly. But despite this characteristic traditionalism, the country has undergone significant change in the past 40 years. Since the 1960s, Portugal has evolved from a largely rural and agrarian country into a more urban and industrialized society. This had a far-reaching impact on the traditional ways of the Portuguese. The traditional family structure began to change, and social tensions were brought on by the growing masses of urban workers and by the abandonment of traditional rural livelihoods in exchange for city jobs.

The 1974 revolution showed that the Portuguese were ready to shed the somber legacy of almost five decades of dictatorship, and move toward a more pluralistic, democratic, and modern society. Membership in the European Union further contributed to modernizing

47

Portuguese men enjoy a peaceful moment at a harbor.

Portugal, not only its infrastructure and economy, but also cultural values. These influences are for the most part regarded as a welcome change, and most Portuguese believe that their country greatly benefited from EU membership. Portuguese Nobel Prize winner José Saramago perhaps best expressed this process of change his home country was (and is) experiencing, when he wrote in *Journey to Portugal*: "Every place I passed through there was a piece of old Portugal bidding farewell to the traveler I was, an ancient Portugal which was beginning, finally, while still doubting whether it wanted to or not, to move towards the 20th century."

During these years of rapid transformation the Portuguese have proven to be an adaptable people who adjusted to these changes with admirable patience and perseverance. More astonishing still, they were mostly able to preserve their traditions and the way of life dear to them. Young people today are more modern, educated, and worldly than their parents, but many of them still partake in the traditional activities that are part of their unique cultural heritage. And despite the trend toward urbanization, not all young Portuguese like the modern urban life. A friend of mine in his early twenties told me that he could never leave the place where he grew up. "I love the calmness of my village," he said.

NEIGHBORS BUT POLES APART

Many foreigners assume that Portugal and Spain are very similar, since they share the same geographic space. Portugal's history is assumed to be the same as that of Spain, and it is often believed that Spanish is also the national language of Portugal. Well, all of the above assumptions are wrong. Even though both countries share a common early history, from Celtic settlers to the drawn-out reconquest during the Middle Ages, Portugal and Spain are today distinctly different countries and cultures. Since Portugal's independence almost 900 years ago, the two countries have nurtured separate identities and have developed their own language and traditions.

Although the Spanish and Portuguese people recognize a certain kinship, their relations are much more based on rivalry than on alliance. It is remembered by all Portuguese that it was the Spanish rule over Portugal from 1580–1640 that put an end to Portugal's Golden Age, which has never since returned. And this age-old rivalry, fought out between kings and armies of foot soldiers and lonesome caravels on the world's vast oceans, still continues to a certain extent to this day, even during this period of prolonged peace, open borders, and a common market and currency. While it is no longer the Spanish military invasions that are feared, the Portuguese are today concerned about a Spanish takeover of the Portuguese economy. It is still the old David and Goliath rivalry that remains alive between the two nations.

Visitors to both countries will quickly realize that it is not only historical rivalry that separates the two countries. The Spanish and Portuguese mentality and way of life are also very different. The Spanish are much more Mediterranean in their extrovertedness, their food, and their customs. They observe the *siesta*, while the Portuguese simply have a lunch break, and both countries have different meal times. The Spanish temperament is livelier than that of the more reserved Portuguese, and musical rhythms are also faster and more passionate in Spain. Just comparing the best-known music traditions in Spain and Portugal gives an insight into the differences between the national souls of the two Iberian countries. The flamenco is passionate, extroverted, and rhythmic, whereas Portugal's fado is melancholic, introverted, and lyrical. Even bullfights have evolved differently, and are much less bloody and dramatic in Portugal than in Spain. In Portugal it is prohibited to kill the bull in the arena.

If you talk to them about their relationship with each other and about their differences, both Spaniards and Portuguese will explain to you in detail how, why, and in what ways the two countries have been different, are different, and will always be different. Quite often a number of proverbs are used to illustrate this point. The best-known Portuguese saying is doubtlessly, *"Em Espanha, nem bons ventos nem bons casamentos"* (In Spain, neither good winds nor good marriages). This proverb refers to the fateful consequences of intermarriage between the royal houses of Spain and Portugal, which led to Portugal's annexation by Spain in 1580. A Portuguese friend explained to me that the winds coming from Spain bring frost and damage the crops. Likewise, the Spanish saying, *"Menos mal, que nos queda Portugal"* (It's not so bad, since there's always Portugal) suggests that no matter how bad things are in Spain, there is always Portugal, where things are worse.

The differences between the Spanish and Portuguese culture and mentality are also noticeable in other areas, such as religion, painting, and architecture, and to discuss these aspects in detail would go beyond the scope of this book. It is interesting to note however, that despite these differences Portugal and Spain have more in common with each other than with the rest of Europe. José Saramago admirably expressed this notion in the novel *The Stone Raft*. In this metaphorical tale, the Iberian Peninsula breaks off from Europe, due to some unforeseen geological event, and slowly drifts out into the ocean toward an uncertain transatlantic destiny. The geographical dislocation in Saramago's novel seems to be an inevitable consequence of a cultural and historical separation from continental Europe that probably began with the Moorish invasion in the 8th century and has survived to this day. The novel was first published in 1986, the year Portugal and Spain joined the European Community, as if to suggest that the Iberian Peninsula was not entirely certain about its destiny in a unified Europe. Today of course, both countries are committed to a common future within the EU, although they maintain their peculiar national characteristics.

FAMILY LIFE

The Pillar of Society

Without a doubt, the family is the most important social unit in Portuguese society, and family life still plays an essential role in the lives of the Portuguese. The traditional Portuguese family is patriarchal, with the father and husband as the head of the family. Under Salazar, only the head of the family could vote, which was the husband in most cases. During this time, the family, together with the church, was considered one of the fundamental elements of Portuguese society, and a marriage joined by the church was considered permanent. The husband was the main provider and took care of family matters outside the home, while the responsibility of the wife and mother rarely extended beyond the domestic sphere. Traditionally the extended family not only included relatives but also godparents, which had a very important role in Portuguese family life in the past. Godparents were often selected to help with the upbringing of a child and also to provide financial assistance for education, if necessary. While this tradition is no longer as important as in the past, godparents are still part of family life, especially in rural Portugal.

Changing Times

Several factors have contributed to changing the traditional structure of the Portuguese family. When the Portuguese, especially men, began to emigrate in large numbers after World War II, women took on greater responsibilities at home during their absence. They worked on the farms and acted as the head of the family, which also gave them the right to vote. In the 1960s, increased emigration as well as migration trends toward urban areas further changed family life. An increasing number of people began to leave their hometowns in search for better work in Portugal's cities or abroad, and the traditional extended family of rural areas was gradually replaced by the urban nuclear family.

As the job market expanded, more and more women entered the work force. Today women provide a considerable percentage of the household income and the husband is no longer the only breadwinner in the family. Young couples also get married later and have children later in life compared to their parents. Since the 1974 revolution family planning and better access to birth control have resulted in a much smaller number of children per family. The number of children per couple dropped from 3.1 in 1960 to 1.5 in 2000. And as parenthood outside wedlock has become more accepted, more and more young couples decide to keep an informal relationship instead of marriage. As women have entered the work force in large numbers, economic considerations no longer play a significant role in prolonging marriages. The 1976 constitution also made divorce universally accessible, and the divorce rate has climbed sharply since then, from about 1% in the early 1970s to 32% in 2000.

The younger generation today has considerably more freedom with regard to marriage than their parents or grandparents did. In the past, marriages were sometimes arranged to better the economic situation of two families or to increase property, but young people are today free to marry whom they wish. The old courting traditions are no longer observed, and young women are no longer accompanied by older relatives when they go out to socialize. Young people today also have it much easier than their parents to meet people of the opposite sex, and they engage in group activities with both young men and women. Some of the old mentalities remain alive in rural areas, but for the most part, the changes in family life are noticeable everywhere and are today part of modern life in Portugal.

Friendship

> *"Amigos e livros querem-se poucos e bons."*
> (Of friends and books we want few and good ones.)
> —Portuguese saying

The Portuguese are a sociable people who place high importance on family life and their circle of friends. This circle of intimate relationships is closely knit, and family life and activities are considered a private affair, only open to relatives and very close friends. The Portuguese are introverted and do not quickly call someone a friend. Friendships are formed over time, through extended companionship and shared experiences. But once friendships are formed they are considered to be strong and longlasting ties, and close friends will be treated as part of the family. How people interact and make friends depends very much on where they live. Social life in rural Portugal is much more transparent than in urban areas. Everyone knows everyone, and usually everyone talks about everyone. Young people live close to each other and see each other in school; neighboring women meet at the market and chat on the street while doing needlework; their husbands may know each other from the barber shop or run into each other at night at the local *tasca* for a glass of wine. On one hand this familiarity promotes friendship and companionship, but on the other hand individuals do not have the same liberties as they have in cities. After a drunken night out on the town a young man may soon have a reputation in a village. Similarly, a single woman with a child out of wedlock is much more easily the subject of gossip in a small town than in a city.

Love Relationships

In general, relationships usually form within close social circles, as is the case with friendships. Group life is very important to the young Portuguese. Few young people engage in individual activities. Young people meet their peers in groups, often in parks, cafés, bars, or other common meeting places. Especially after school and at night, bakeries, cafés, and bars fill up with groups of friends who gather for a chat and refreshment. The social structure of the university environment with

A couple enjoy a quiet moment at a river park near the Vasco de Gama Bridge.

the student association of each department often forming close social circles is doubtlessly another very important environment for the social life of young Portuguese. Out of these group activities, be they in the context of a village, school, or university, emerge couples who engage in a *namoro* (love relationship). Since many young people live with their parents and have little privacy at home, it is quite common to see couples hugging on park benches and in other public places. The process of courtship used to be very traditional and had to follow established rules. Nowadays, when young people want to have a relationship, the boyfriend no longer has to ask the girl's father.

Marriage

When a relationship advances and becomes more committed, a young couple may decide to get married and they will then announce their *noivado* (engagement). The man traditionally presents an engagement ring to the woman, and asks the father for the hand of his daughter. A short time before the wedding it is common for the groom to get together with his friends for a last night out as a bachelor. This bachelor's party is known as the *despedida de solteiro*. Similarly, the bride gets together with her girlfriends, either for an afternoon tea or a dinner. The Portuguese are a traditional people, and for many the wedding is the most important event in their lives.

How the wedding ceremony and the reception are organized depends on the economic situation of the two families, but regardless of the financial background, a wedding is always a merry celebration with food, music, and dance. Most Portuguese prefer a wedding ceremony at a church, which is usually decorated with white flowers. At the end of the ceremony, when leaving the church, the young couple is greeted with flower petals and rice, and as is customary in many other countries, the bride throws her bridal bouquet at her unmarried girlfriends. Wedding lists at stores have become increasingly popular, so wedding guests can coordinate their presents with the needs and wishes of the young couple.

Children

Although the Portuguese have fewer children today than a generation ago, they are still family-oriented. The birth of a child is always a reason for a celebration. Both parents care for their children, but mothers usually take most of the responsibility for raising their offspring. The Portuguese are very tolerant toward children and treat them with much affection. As a family-oriented people, the Portuguese also have a lot of time for their children. Rarely will you see a child being ushered along or hurried by a parent. The Portuguese also bring their children with them wherever they go. They take their children to dinners at restaurants and often let them stay up late on outings and get-togethers. Children in Portugal generally enjoy a lot of freedom to play, both in public and private. They sing, run around, chatter, and scream in public without anyone taking offense.

The Twilight Years

Most elderly people have close contact with the younger generation, and in the countryside they often live in the same household. Portugal's retired population leads a very social life, and no matter where you are, there are elderly people that populate public gathering places. Men meet at parks for an afternoon chat or sit at tables playing dominoes or cards. Women, especially in rural areas, stay closer to home and sit in front of their doorsteps for lively conversation with their friends and neighbors, while busily doing embroidery, knitting, stitching, or lacework. Since pensions are meager in Portugal, a good number of old people work to earn a little money on the side. In the countryside many old people still work in the fields or in their vegetable plot, and women sell produce or fish at local markets. In cities elderly people sell knickknacks on the street, and retired men proffer lottery tickets by announcing the drawings in a loud, repetitive singsong voice.

A group of senior citizens plays cards in a park.

Death and Dying

In a country where the family is an important part of life, the loss of a relative is a tragic event. Catholic rites accompany the ill or dying, and a priest usually administers the sacrament of anointing of the sick. On the day of the funeral there is usually a mass, after which the invited guests make their condolences. Family members bring flowers or wreaths. The immediate family usually wears black, but the traditional rules about mourning are no longer strictly observed. In the past, both widows and women whose husbands worked abroad were expected to wear black every day. While most elderly widows in rural areas still observe this tradition, this is no longer the case in cities. Dead family members are especially remembered every year on November 2, the Dia dos Fiéis Defuntos (Day of the Dead).

SENTIMENTS AND PERCEPTIONS

Saudade—the National Sentiment

> *"Que me quereis, perpétuas saudades?*
> *Com que esperança ainda me enganais?*
> *Que o tempo que se vai não torna mais,*
> *e se torna, não tornam as idades."*
> (What do you want from me, perpetual saudades?
> With what hope do you still deceive me?
> Time that passes does not return,
> And if it did, age does not turn back.)
> —Luís de Camões, *Sonetos*

Saudade is the longing for the better days of the past and for far-away friends and loved ones, or as some say, the longing of the seafarers for their distant homeland. Whatever its origins, *saudade* is a deeply felt emotion that has accompanied the Portuguese since the country's remote beginnings. *Saudade* is derived from the Latin word *solum*, which means alone. The word's origin seems to suggest that for the Portuguese, the feelings of melancholy and nostalgia are related to or caused by being alone or lonely. A Portuguese dictionary explains *saudade* as "a more or less melancholic sentiment of incompleteness," which again hints at the word's origin in the Latin "alone."

The Portuguese say that *saudade* exists in no other language and believe that this emotion of nostalgic longing is unique to the Portuguese experience. It is true that the term *saudade* does not have an exact synonym in other languages today, but it is also true that the sentiment of *saudade* is shared by all humans. What is unique to the Portuguese, however, is the importance of *saudade* both on an individual and collective level. *Saudade* is not only an emotion felt by individuals when they miss distant loved ones or their home country, but also a cultural and historical reality, based on the notion that the country's great past lies all too far in the distant past. *Saudade* for the Portuguese is therefore very much a symbol of national identity, and the Portuguese talk about *saudade* not only as a sentiment, but as a prized possession and national characteristic, as if it were the main jewel in the crown of the national soul.

Saudade also plays an essential role in the Portuguese arts and is often the main theme and inspiration in music and poetry. From the medieval minstrel songs to the romantic poet Almeida Garrett, and from the great Camões to the modernist Pessoa and the nostalgic fado tunes, *saudade* is an essential component of Portuguese music and literature.

Sebastianism and Portugal's Unfulfilled Destiny

> *"Cumpriu-se o Mar e o Império se desfez*
> *Senhor, falta cumprir-se Portugal."*
> (The Sea fulfilled itself and the Empire came undone
> Lord, what remains is for Portugal to fulfill itself.)
> —Fernando Pessoa, *Mensagem*

It was first during the Spanish dominance from 1580–1640 that the myth about Portugal's great destiny became popular. After the disappearance of King Sebastião on the battlefield of Alcázarquivir in 1578, the belief in his glorious return became increasingly popular among the Portuguese and remained alive in people's minds as a notion of hope for a long time. The Jesuit father António Vieira (1608–1697) expanded this popular myth of King Sebastião's return into a full-fledged messianic ideology, which became known as *Sebastianismo* (Sebastianism). Based on the legend of Christ's apparition to Portugal's first king Afonso Henriques, Vieira elaborated on the importance of the Portuguese nation in establishing Christ's kingdom on earth, which he called the Fifth Empire, successor of the four great empires of antiquity. He prophesied that King Sebastião, the Hidden One, would return and reestablish the great Portuguese empire. Sebastianism may seem like another one of Portugal's many historical myths, but the notion of Portugal's special destiny has been elaborated by theologists, historians, and politicians alike and has played a dominant role in Portuguese discourse on history for hundreds of years. Pessoa's poem *Mensagem*, the only one that was published during his lifetime, is perhaps the most notable literary work of the 20th century dedicated to this messianic hope that Portugal's destiny may still be fulfilled. In a recent book on postmodern culture (*Pela mão de Alice: o social e o político na pós-modernidade*, 1994), sociologist Boaventura de Sousa Santos found it necessary to remind his compatriots that Portugal really has no destiny, but only a history, just like every other nation.

Fado, Fátima e Futebol

Commonly known as the three "F"s, referring to fado, Fátima and *futebol* (soccer), this term is today often used to describe the cultural reality of Portugal during the Salazar years, when fado, religion, and soccer were the only officially sanctioned diversions of a people oppressed by a dictatorial regime. But even though three decades have passed since the end of the dictatorship, fado, Fátima, and *futebol* still largely sum up Portugal's national passions.

Fado, with its nostalgic and sad undertone, is one of the most authentic expressions of the Portuguese people. Ever since its beginnings in the 19th century, the mournful fado tunes have given a voice to the sorrows of the Portuguese people, who sing about their loves and their fate in life. As one famous fado says: "*Tudo isto existe, tudo isto é triste, tudo isto é fado...*" (All this exists, all this is sad, all this is fado...). It is hardly coincidental that the name of Portugal's most typical folk music form also means fate or destiny. Fado is not only a musical genre, but also a state of mind, a way of experiencing life and looking at the world. It is an attitude of accepting one's fate in life, and in the traditional fado music the musicians and the audience often commiserate their lot in life. What makes fado so popular with the common people are not only the heartfelt lyrics, but also its informal performances that allow people to sing along or even perform. Fado is emotionally charged, and many famous fado tunes are very personal stories about love and the ups and downs of life. When I went to listen to fado at Lisbon's small *tascas*, I soon realized that this wasn't music for people who wanted to listen, chat, laugh, and have a good time. It is music that makes people become introspective and feel their own fado. Before a fado performance, a presenter always asks for absolute silence, and then he dims the light before the musicians start to play. Fado is sad music, and listening to fado is a serious matter.

The large sanctuary at Fátima sums up another essential element of Portuguese culture: religion. Fátima is Portugal's largest pilgrimage site, and hundreds of thousands of pilgrims arrive from every corner of Portugal. They come to the site of the apparition of the Virgin Mary to pay vows and pray for help. It is amazing how much effort and time the Portuguese put into their religious practices, and Fátima epitomizes this devotion.

Soccer is Portugal's most popular spectator sport and a true national passion. Although actual attendance at stadiums is modest, soccer fans really reveal their passion at night in front of a TV at a tavern. Leaning against a bar with a glass of wine in hand is the Portuguese soccer fan's favorite position, from which he can comfortably follow a game by his favorite team and engage in heated discussions with his peers.

In Portugal, soccer assumes much larger proportions than a game. As in other countries where soccer is popular, soccer fields are substitute battlegrounds where national honors are lost and won. The vocabulary is charged with war terminology and emotions can run very high, especially during a game involving the national team. During such a game the happiness of the entire nation is at stake, and, as the disastrous performance at the 2002 World Cup has shown, can almost lead to national depression. Although it is difficult to establish

a connection to soccer, it is a fact that the national mood thermometer drastically declined after the team's bad performance in Japan and Korea. Opinion polls for the rest of 2002 showed the Portuguese increasingly pessimistic about the economy and their country in general. While successes in soccer obviously do not directly boost a lagging economy, a better performance during the World Cup would have doubtlessly injected a little bit of much-needed optimism into the Portuguese soul. But within this typically Portuguese pessimism there always remains room for hope, and so everyone believes that the results of the next soccer championships, the Euro 2004 held in Portugal and the 2006 World Cup in Germany, will doubtlessly be better, or won't they?

The Portuguese about Themselves

The Portuguese have mixed feelings about their country and culture. On one hand they praise their food, wine, and the beauty of their country, but when it comes to social, political, and cultural issues, most opinions are critical and negative. One almost gets the impression that the Portuguese are not particularly proud of themselves or their country. No doubt, the Portuguese have a national pride and have plenty of good things to say about their country, but they seem to battle with the awareness of the relative insignificance of Portugal on a political, economic, and cultural level. Opinions vary, of course, but the urban and more educated population is very critical of the state of affairs in Portugal and often compares their country with the richer and more advanced European nations. "Even Greece is now ahead of us," I was often told when talking to people about the state of affairs in Portugal. But on a more visceral level, I have heard a lot of people say good things about their country. As an old ticket vendor in Porto told me: "Portugal is great. The food is good, the wine is good, and the women are good too!"

The Portuguese about Foreigners

> *"Estrangeiro sempre é estrangeiro."*
> (A foreigner is always a foreigner.)
>
> —Portuguese saying.

What the Portuguese think of foreigners depends on where they are from and what they are doing in Portugal. Tourists may be seen as an annoyance at times, but they also spend a lot of money in Portugal and are overall welcome and treated with courtesy and respect. Since many Portuguese worked abroad at one time or another, mostly in Germany, Switzerland, and France, they are eager to show that they liked the country they worked in and that they know the language. The attitude toward those who come to Portugal to work is somewhat different. These are people from countries even poorer than Portugal, which gives the Portuguese some reason to treat them with less respect. This is often reflected in the poorly paid jobs that most immigrants work in, regardless if they are from Eastern Europe,

Africa, or Brazil. Although Portugal's historic seafaring exploits are often used as an example to explain the tolerance of the Portuguese toward foreigners and strangers, the daily reality reveals that the Portuguese are not quite as tolerant or fond of immigrants. With unemployment on the rise public opinion has also recently shifted toward restricting immigration, since immigrants may take jobs away from the Portuguese.

Chapter Five

A DEEPLY ROOTED FAITH

*"E glória singular do Reino de Portugal que só ele, entre
todos os do mundo, foi fundado e instituído por Deus."*
(It is the single glory of the kingdom of Portugal that it
alone among all others in the world was founded and
instituted by God.)

—Father António Vieira (1608–1697)

The Christian faith was instrumental to the founding of the Portuguese
kingdom. On the eve of the battle of Ourique in 1139, so legend has
it, the Portuguese Count Afonso Henriques had a dream, in which he
saw an apparition of Christ, revealing his five wounds. "In you and
your descendants I will found my kingdom," were the Savior's words,
and he also told Henriques to put the symbol of five discs (arranged

symmetrically, somewhat like a cross) on his shield, in memory of the five wounds of Christ. These so-called five *quinas* (groups of five coins), together with seven castles that symbolize the cities conquered from the Moors, are still part of Portugal's flag. On the day of the battle, Henriques rode off into a sure victory for the Portuguese army and soon after began to call himself king of Portugal. Although just a legend, this event deeply shaped the history and sense of destiny of the Portuguese nation: Portugal was not just any kingdom, it was established by God's will. The Portuguese saw the existence of their nation as an act of divine intervention and took the defense of Christianity and of their nation very seriously. This conviction gave rise to a religious zeal and deeply rooted faith that helped defeat the Moors and later lent itself well to the Inquisition, whose oppressive rule lasted into the early 19th century. The Catholic Church remained one of Portugal's most powerful institutions until well into the 20th century, and had a significant influence on public and private life, which is still noticeable to some degree today.

CATHOLICISM TODAY

After the 1974 revolution, Portugal experienced a trend toward secularization. The 1976 constitution instituted the separation between State and Church, which remains intact until today. Although around 94% of the Portuguese population declare themselves Roman Catholic, they no longer practice Catholicism in the same way as previous generations. As the Portuguese have emerged from a rural and largely illiterate society into a more urban and educated people over the past few decades, religious practice has declined and is no longer an integral part of life. Young people, especially, have little interest in the Catholic Church and religion. Only about a third of the population attend mass regularly, mostly older people and women. But despite the increasing secularization of Portuguese society, the opinions of the Church still play a vital role in public life. The voice of the Church may not always be obeyed, but people pay attention to what their religious leaders have to say. Bishops, cardinals, and the Pope are regularly quoted in the media, and they still yield a significant influence as opinion-makers.

RITUALS TO LIVE BY

> *"Colchas ricas nas janelas,*
> *pétalas soltas no chão.*
> *Almas crentes, povo rude*
> *anda a fé pelas vielas:*
> *é dia da procissão*
> *da senhora da saúde."*
> (Rich bedspreads in the windows,
> loose petals on the ground.
> Believing souls, crude people
> Faith walks through the alleys:
> It is the day of the procession
> of the lady of health.")
>   —from the fado *Há festa na Mouraria*, lyrics by
>   A. Amargo; music by A. Duarte

Catholic traditions have shaped Portugal since its remote beginnings, and the Portuguese have strong historical and cultural ties to the Catholic Church. Although many people no longer practice their faith regularly, the lives of most Portuguese are accompanied by the rituals of the Catholic Church. Family life as well as the nation's cultural life are strongly centered around Catholic traditions. These practices include baptism, first communion, confession, weddings, and funerals, as well as the many Catholic holidays, pilgrimages, and festivals celebrated on a regional and national level.

Childhood Within the Church
Baptism is the first official Catholic rite in the life of a newborn.

Before the child is baptized, parents traditionally ask relatives or close friends to become the child's godparents. The godparents' role is to help in the child's upbringing and provide encouragement, but also to possibly take the role of the parents in an emergency. The first communion is another important religious ceremony, during which a child (between six and eight years old) participates for the first time in the Eucharist. For many children, mostly in rural areas, growing up also means taking part in many religious festivals. They dress up as angels or biblical figures and play an important role in processions all over Portugal. The sacrament of Confirmation usually takes place when the child enters adolescence, and reaffirms the young person's faith and commitment to the Church.

Marriage

Marriage is one of the seven sacraments of the Catholic Church, and still has a strong symbolic importance in Portugal. Although young

Children are a major part of religious processions in Portugal.

people today are not nearly as religious as previous generations, the blessing of their lifelong union by a priest is still important for many. Almost two thirds of all weddings in Portugal take place in a church.

Illness and Death

It is in illness and death where the Catholic faith reveals its importance in people's lives. The sacrament of anointing the sick is an important rite intended to provide spiritual peace, support, and encouragement for the ill. The priest anoints the sick or dying person with oil and prays for recovery, God willing. After the death of a family member a nightlong wake is usually held, either at the home of the deceased or at a funeral home. Funerals are held a few days later, and a priest or family member may hold a brief eulogy. Often a death mass is read in the cemetery chapel before the funeral, and depending on family traditions there may be another mass on the 7th and 30th day of the person's death, to which friends and family are invited.

Most funerals in Portugal are still traditional burials. Cremation is rare and is only now starting to become more frequent, often due to the lack of space in cemeteries. Many tombs are built aboveground, and large cemeteries resemble veritable necropolises—cities of the dead. The more lavish tombs resemble medieval castles, Manueline churches, or classical temples, and are sometimes adorned by weeping angels or melancholic maidens. Dia dos Fiéis Defuntos (on November 2) is the day when people remember the deceased and attend to their graves. Tombs are swept, and coffins are polished and decorated with clean, white cloths. Photographs and figures of saints that are usually part of the tomb interior, are dusted, and bright fresh flowers are put next to them. This is the only time of year when the drab and gray cemeteries take on a new life with colorful flowers on every grave and inside every tomb. The flowers' fresh fragrance, so it seems, helps to dissipate for a short while the somber atmosphere that is so aptly expressed in an inscription at the cemetery entrance in Ourém:

> *"Ancorados neste porto*
> *Livres já da tempestade*
> *Os mortos só pedem lágrimas,*
> *Uma prece, uma saudade."*
> (Anchored at this port,
> Free already of life's tempest,
> The dead only ask for tears,
> A prayer, a nostalgic memory.)

RELIGIOUS PRACTICES

Daily Signs of Faith

That many Portuguese still take their Catholic faith seriously is revealed in daily life, when people's religious sentiments are expressed in many small ways. People may say a prayer before eating, or make the sign of the cross to ask for divine protection. It is also quite common to invoke divine protection in conversation and in a variety of different situations. I remember a blind beggar in Braga who sat outside a church every day and repeated the same litany all day long. He was asking for alms and was invoking the protection of St. Luzia, the protector of eyesight, for passersby. Likewise, Santa Barbara might be called for protection during a thunderstorm. Phrases like *"graças a Deus"* (thank God) or *"se Deus quiser"* (God willing), which are heard frequently, are for most people not merely a manner of speech, but a sincere gesture that should be taken seriously. At a bus station in a small town in Trás-os-Montes, I asked about a bus connection and told the vendor that I would return the following day to purchase the ticket. "God willing, I will be here tomorrow," the old man replied several times, suggesting that his well-being entirely depended on the will of God. I was glad to find him in the same spot the next day, listening to his little transistor radio. There are also many proverbs that express the traditional faith of the people and reveal a slight fatalism so characteristic of the Portuguese. Some of these sayings, used mostly by the older generation, include: *"dá Deus o frio conforme a roupa"* (God sends the cold according to one's clothing) or *"o futuro a Deus pertence"* (The future belongs to God).

Honoring the Saints

Saints were considered important intermediaries between common sinners and God, which has led to a widespread and popular cult of saints. Till today saints are asked to intercede with God for a variety of problems and concerns. On the dangerous seafaring expeditions during the Age of Discovery, for example, navigators brought along with them the images of saints they were devoted to. Even today the Portuguese ask for divine protection when traveling. St. Christopher, the patron saint of travelers, not only accompanies many motorists as an amulet dangling from the rearview mirror, but also greets travelers in the form of a monumental statue at Lisbon's airport.

Saints not only help individuals in times of need, but they are also the protectors of entire communities. Every village, town, and city in Portugal has a patron saint, or a saint the local church is dedicated to. For centuries the patron saints were honored by festivals organized by the parish to ensure the continued protection and prosperity of their communities and the favor of the saints. This tradition is still widely practiced today, not only to invoke the saints' protection through masses and processions, but also (or mainly) to get together with friends and family for a lively feast. Folk music, dances, and challenge songs (men and women taking turns singing songs with impromptu lyrics that poke fun at each other) are performed during such festivals, and games, raffles, and contests take place on the fairgrounds. The amount of collective and individual effort that goes into religious festivals is truly astounding. People make decorations, sew costumes, and practice songs months before the actual event, and then carry heavy statues of saints around town during lengthy processions. While there is certainly a showy and gaudy element to some festivals, many are deeply religious events, where the devotion of the townspeople to their patron saint becomes obvious in the sincerity and festive atmosphere of the procession.

Pilgrimages and Vows

People ask the saints for help for a variety of reasons, and most saints have special powers attributed to them for certain areas of life. St. Anthony is known to help people find lost items, St. John is invoked to help find a marriage partner, and St. Peter is the protector of fishermen. The most common form of asking a saint for help is to make a votive offering, give alms, or say prayers. When in serious distress, people may make a vow, in which they make a special promise to a saint should their prayer be answered. Paying a vow can be a simple gesture such as lighting a votive candle at a shrine. Another way to thank a saint for helping or ask for help is to make a pilgrimage to a sanctuary devoted to the saint. Pilgrimages are the most devout of public expressions of faith and there are many sanctuaries all over Portugal with important annual pilgrimages. See the festival calendar in Chapter 8 for more details. People usually visit the shrine of a saint as part of a vow and to thank the saint for intervening on their behalf. At pilgrimage sites people leave votive gifts, often in the form of wax or wood replicas of the healed body parts, or photographs with a short message thanking the saint.

THE VIRGIN OF FÁTIMA

Fátima is Portugal's largest pilgrimage sanctuary and epitomizes in many ways the religious sentiment of the Portuguese people. Fátima is the site of a series of apparitions of the Virgin Mary, which allegedly occurred in 1917. Each year the sanctuary attracts over 4 million pilgrims from all over the world. The most popular pilgrimages take place on the 12th and 13th day of the month from May through October, in remembrance of the original six apparitions of the virgin during this period. The story is as follows: on May 13, 1917, while watching a small flock of sheep near the village of Fátima, three

The basilica at Fátima.

shepherd children saw a flash of light, from which emerged a bright light that rested on a tree. In it appeared the Holy Virgin, with a white rosary in her hands, the way the Virgin of Fátima is still portrayed in statues and images today. She asked the children to pray for peace in the world and promised to appear on the same day during the following months. The apparitions were repeated in the following five months. During these apparitions the Virgin shared several secret messages with one of the children, Lúcia. Two of them dealt with World War I and the Bolshevik revolution. The third message however, was not revealed until Pope John Paul II visited Fátima in

2000. Apparently it had been a prophesy of the assassination attempt on the Pope in 1981. The last apparition was on October 13, 1917, when the so-called "miracle of the sun" was witnessed by around 70,000 pilgrims. According to eyewitnesses, the sky suddenly darkened and the sun moved across the sky in a large circle. It was not until 13 years later, after a long and careful investigation, that the Catholic Church officially acknowledged the apparitions.

Due to the rapidly growing number of pilgrims, the original small chapel built on the site of the apparition was replaced by an imposing basilica that took 25 years to construct. The actual heart of the sanctuary is the small, modern Chapel of the Apparitions, which was erected on the site where the Virgin first appeared to the children. It also houses the famous statue of the Virgin, whose copy can be bought in different sizes at the many stalls that surround the sanctuary.

Days before the popular pilgrimages on the 13th day of each month from May to October, the roads to Fátima are crowded with thousands of pilgrims who walk to the sanctuary from all over Portugal. These are modern pilgrims, equipped with reflective vests and support teams in automobiles, but their faith remains unchanged. Just as in 1917 these people come to Fátima to pay vows, pray, or ask the Virgin for help. The highlights of the pilgrimages are outdoor masses in the courtyard of the basilica, and processions of the image of the Virgin of Fátima. During the last night of every pilgrimage cycle, the large square in front of the basilica turns into a sea of light, as tens of thousands of pilgrims hold up candles while attending outdoor mass.

CATHOLIC CELEBRATIONS AND TRADITIONS

Portugal is rich in religious traditions, many of them of pagan origin, which were later adopted by the Catholic Church. Even the main Catholic holidays contain pagan elements often related to solstice and harvest celebrations. Below is a short description of how the most important Catholic celebrations are commemorated in Portugal.

Carnaval (Mardi Gras)

Carnaval is usually celebrated on the last weekend before Quarta Feira de Cinzas (Ash Wednesday), beginning with Domingo Gordo (Shrove Sunday), and continuing until Terça Feira de Carnaval (Shrove Tuesday). The Portuguese carnaval is a very folkloric and unique event often with age-old pagan elements. In the mountainous northeast, so-called *caretos* (devilish figures) parade through town and form an important part of the carnaval tradition. During carnaval people play pranks on each other, throw flour or water at the crowd on the street, and seem to take as much advantage as possible of the saying that *"no carnaval ninguém leva a mal"* (during carnaval nobody takes offense). The *entrudo* is another popular carnaval tradition throughout Portugal. It is a large straw puppet that is carried through the streets in a lively procession on Ash Wednesday and then either buried or burned. In recent years Brazilian-style carnaval celebrations with samba schools and large processions have become increasingly popular, especially from Lisbon south to the Algarve. In northern Portugal, carnaval is mostly celebrated in the traditional way.

Quaresma (Lent)

The days of Lent between Ash Wednesday and Easter Sunday are a period marked by penitence. After the revelry of carnaval, the mood changes quickly on Ash Wednesday. In some regions people dressed up as *a Morte e Diabos* (Death and Devils) parade through the streets to remind revelers and passersby that Lent, the period of penitence, has indeed begun. Lent is not only a time of personal penitence, but also a time when people pray for the delivery of the souls in purgatory. This ritual usually takes place at night on certain days during Lent, sometimes even in public, when prayers are sung in deliberately distorted voices.

Páscoa (Holy Week and Easter)

Easter is the most important cycle of festivities of the ecclesiastic year, and has special importance in a Catholic country such as Portugal. Easter celebrations begin with the blessing of the palm branches on Palm Sunday and last until Easter Sunday. The Via Dolorosa or Via Sacra (Stations of the Cross) is an important ritual during Holy Week. The faithful relive the Passion of Christ, from his judgment to his death, by visiting 14 different stations (mostly crosses or small chapels) where they meditate about the Passion. Good Friday is the day of the procession of the Lord's Burial, during which a piece of the consecrated host, symbolizing the body of Christ, is carried in a procession to a symbolic tomb placed on an altar, where it remains until Sunday, the day of Resurrection. The *O Enterro do Bacalhau* (burial of the bacalhau) is a ritual that marks the end of Lent, during which *bacalhau* (dried salted cod) is one of the main staple foods, since meat is prohibited. This ceremonial burial of a piece of codfish takes place on Holy Saturday. Other Easter traditions such as the Queima de Judas (the Burning of Judas) also celebrate the end of Lent. This rite includes the burning of a straw puppet representing Judas. On Easter Sunday people all over Portugal celebrate the procession of the resurrection and indulge in a festive meal, since it marks the end of the fasting period. Some towns hold lively fairs with music and dance after the Easter mass.

Natal (Christmas)

Christmas is a family feast that follows age-old Portuguese traditions. In homes people sometimes put up small Christmas decorations with branches of fir trees. Families also put up a small nativity scene on Christmas Eve. This is also customary for most parishes, where life-size nativity scenes are put up at the entrances of most churches or in churchyards. In many small towns and villages you will still find the old tradition of burning a tree or tree trunk on Christmas Eve in front of the village or town church. In other areas there is simply a large bonfire that is lit at the time of the midnight mass. In recent decades, Christmas has become increasingly internationalized, and some old traditions are giving way to plastic Christmas trees and images of Santa Claus in his bright red costume. Although cut Christmas trees in homes are rare, it is quite common to adorn life trees on streets and squares with Christmas decorations.

Christmas in Portugal is very much centered around food. The traditional meal on Christmas Eve, known as *consoada* or *ceia de natal*, is mostly a *bacalhau* dish, often served with potatoes and cabbage, but in some regions pork is preferred. Afterwards families gather around the nativity scene to sing Christmas carols and exchange gifts. The midnight mass usually forms the end of the Christmas Eve celebrations. Many people also attend mass on the morning of Christmas and then indulge in a sumptuous Christmas dinner. Everywhere in Portugal during the holiday season people eat a special cake called *bolo rei* (cake of the king), a sweet yeast bread topped with colorful candied fruit. This cake is popular from Christmas through Epiphany, and is enjoyed in every family. Two surprises await those who eat the cake: a small gift (a pendant or something similar), and a broad bean are inside the cake. Whoever gets the slice with the gift gets to keep it, and the one who gets the bean has to bring the *bolo rei* for the holidays the following year.

OTHER RELIGIONS

Portugal's Catholicism has been deeply ingrained in the national soul for almost a thousand years, and the practice of other faiths was prohibited under the Inquisition and later openly discouraged. This may be the main reason why there are only a few small congregations of other faiths in Portugal. It- was the 1976 constitution that guaranteed for the first time the right to free religious practice in Portugal. Today, there is a minority of Protestant churches such as Anglicans, Methodists, and Baptists, as well as Jehovah's Witnesses, Mormons, Assemblies of God, and the Universal Church of the Kingdom of God followers. There are also several small Jewish communities and small immigrant congregations of Muslims, Sikhs, Hindus, and other faiths.

FOLK BELIEFS AND SUPERSTITIONS

In addition to Portugal's deeply ingrained Catholic faith, there are age-old traditions of popular folk beliefs that run parallel and sometimes within the teachings of the Church. Folk beliefs often relate to superstitions and irrational fears, and suggest simple remedies and rituals to avert back luck or bring about good fortune. In rural Portugal folk healers still employ magic or superstition to bring about the desired treatment. With Portugal's increased urbanization, some of these practices are beginning to disappear, but in remote areas, especially in northern Portugal, it is not unusual to find people, mostly women, who still practice witchcraft and sorcery, often by using prayers and other elements from the Catholic faith. In many villages there are also practicing healers, magicians, and soothsayers, often engaged in helping the villagers avert evil and deal with illnesses and dangers. Another curious element of folk belief and superstition in Portugal is the so-called *mau olho* or *quebranto* (evil eye), which is the power to bewitch people, mostly children, by just looking at them or giving them too much praise. To avert such a spell, superstition has it that people have to quickly say "May God bless him/her." Another known remedy against witchcraft and the evil eye is to pour salt on the street in the shape of a cross. It is believed that witches are afraid of St. John, and the curse of the evil eye is immediately broken by calling out the name of St. John.

There are also a number of popular superstitions, some of which have Christian roots. Some are uniquely Portuguese, but many are known in other European countries. Among the better known superstitions are those that supposedly bring bad luck or misfortune: Friday the 13th; thirteen people seated at a table; crossed knives at a table; walking under a ladder; opening an umbrella inside the house; leaving keys, scissors, money, or a hat on the bed; exposing babies to moonlight; toasting with water; and many more.

Chapter Six

DO AS THE PORTUGUESE DO

"Em Roma, ser Romano." (In Rome, be a Roman.)
—Portuguese proverb

Portuguese customs and etiquette are somewhat formal, but not in a complicated or ceremonial way. For the most part, foreigners won't take very long to get a basic idea of how to act appropriately in different social situations.

GREETINGS
The Portuguese are formal people, and this is reflected in their greetings and forms of address. A firm and friendly handshake is the

traditional greeting when arriving and departing. When shaking hands people use common phrases such as *bom dia* (good morning), *boa tarde* (good afternoon/evening), or *boa noite* (good night). People who know each other may use an informal greeting such as *olá* (hello). When inquiring about someone's well-being the Portuguese simply ask *tudo bom?* (All is well?) or *como está?* (How are you?) As a general rule, the younger person greets the older, the person lower in rank greets the superior, and the person arriving greets those who are already present. As a sign of good manners, do not greet people with one hand in your pocket or a cigarette in your mouth.

Women either offer their hand in greeting or they may offer a cheek for a kiss, depending on the intimacy and the situation. Kisses are usually given on both cheeks. They are usually just air kisses with the cheeks touching lightly. Among women an embrace and/or kiss is generally more common than a handshake. Light kisses are a common greeting among the younger generation, even among people who don't know each other, but it may be inappropriate to kiss an older woman whom one has just met. When in doubt, unless an older woman offers her cheek, a handshake is perfectly acceptable. Men shake hands in greeting, and male friends often pat each other on the shoulder as well. When introduced to someone, it is customary to shake hands and say *prazer em conhecé-lo* (a pleasure to meet you). When introducing people who do not know each other, the person of lower status is introduced to those of superior status, men are introduced to women, and younger people are introduced to older people. People who know each other usually take leave of each other with a casual *tchau* (from the Italian *ciao*) or *até logo* (see you later). A more formal way of taking leave would be *boa tarde* or *boa noite*. *Adeus* (go with God) can also be used when leaving, but it is usually for situations where the goodbye is more permanent.

FORMS OF ADDRESS

Since the Portuguese are formal and status-conscious, it is important to use the appropriate address in conversation. For anyone other than family members or friends, *senhor* (Sir, Mr.) or *senhora* (Lady, Ms.) is the appropriate formal address. In Portuguese the polite form is expressed in the third person singular. "Would you like a coffee?" is politely expressed as *"O senhor/a senhora quer um café?"* (The Sir/Lady would like a coffee?) Academic titles are always used when they are known, and people may address someone as *senhor doutor* (Mister doctor) or *doutora* (female form), or as *engenheiro* (engineer) or *professor* (professor). To formally address a group the Portuguese say *senhores* (gentlemen) or *senhoras* (ladies), or *senhoras e senhores* (ladies and gentlemen). As a general rule of thumb, the pronoun *tu* (you) is used for family and friends, and *você* (a slightly more formal *you*) is commonly used among equals (such as coworkers or peers). In Portugal *tu* or *você* are usually inappropriate ways to address strangers, unless they are much younger. When intending to show respect, it is best to use the polite address *senhora/senhor*.

IN CONVERSATION

"Fala pouco e bem, ter-te-ão por alguém."
(If you speak little and well, they will take you for someone.)

—Portuguese proverb

One of the first noticeable things about the Portuguese is how much people have time for conversation. Especially in rural Portugal, and even more so in the south, people love to gather in public to chat. People of all ages stand together in small groups at doorways, in squares, in parks, or at cafés, engaged in lively conversation at just about any time of day. Although the Portuguese frequently engage in lively conversations with friends and neighbors, they are not a particularly extroverted people and are somewhat reserved toward strangers. The Portuguese have little ability for small talk and do not

81

easily strike up a conversation with someone they don't know. At the same time they are very polite and do not easily disturb the privacy of strangers by talking to them. As the above-quoted proverb suggests, it shows good manners and elevated status to speak little. This is especially true when talking to strangers. However, things loosen up a bit when sharing a restaurant table for lunch, or after a few glasses of wine at a bar. In these situations conversations arise more naturally.

Conversation Topics

> *"Não fale de cordas em casa de enforcado."*
> (In a hanged man's house, don't talk about ropes.)
> —Portuguese proverb

The Portuguese are private people, and it is inappropriate to ask personal questions about family, income, or work. Personal topics

A group of Portuguese men have an afternoon chat in the park.

such as family or professional life are not readily shared with strangers. These topics are reserved for people of one's own close social circle. There is a decided difference between conversation topics among friends and those among acquaintances and strangers. Naturally, what the Portuguese talk about varies according to social group, age, gender, and region. In general, the Portuguese enjoy talking about the beauty of their hometown or region. While women tend to discuss domestic issues with each other and exchange town gossip, men talk more about soccer and politics. People tend to be very opinionated about political affairs, and in conversation with strangers opinions are shared cautiously. On many occasions, when political topics came up in conversation, people have asked me carefully if I minded their frank opinions. Soccer is another popular conversation topic, and passion runs high among the fans of the different teams. An expatriate friend of mine started a friendly conversation with a Lisbon taxi driver about the Sporting soccer club, without knowing that Lisbon's favorite team is the rival Benfica club. He only realized that this was a bad idea when the driver started to argue with him. Soccer may seem a benign topic to many foreigners, but for the Portuguese it is a national passion. I have sometimes teasingly mentioned the disastrous performance of the Portuguese national team during the 2002 World Cup in Korea/Japan, but it was not well received. Soccer is no laughing matter in Portugal.

Humor

> *"O riso é a mais antiga e ainda mais terrível forma de crítica."*
> (Laughing is the oldest and still the most terrible form of criticism.)
>
> —Eça de Queirós

The Portuguese are a serious people, and meeting someone with a cheerful disposition and a good sense of humor is rare. Perhaps it is the country's long history, with its disappointed hopes, that weighs heavily on the national soul, but humor is not a major form of national expression. The media are serious, newspapers are serious, the music is sad and serious, and so are the great works of Portuguese literature. Television is also serious and the few comical TV programs that exist are rip-offs from abroad.

The Portuguese are not a people who easily laugh about themselves or about anyone else for that matter. They consider it inappropriate to make fun of one another, and are quite afraid of *fazer má figura* (looking bad in public), that is, of being laughed at. Laughing in public seems to be the prerogative of children and adolescents and seems less acceptable than hugging or kissing, probably because of its connotation with making fun of others. Conversations at cafés and bars may be loud and lively, but expressions remain mostly serious and few people laugh in public. This does not mean that the Portuguese are never in a good mood. It just means that they are not as apt in showing joy in public, and that it takes them time to warm up and laugh.

INVITING AND BEING INVITED

> *"A boda ou batizado só vai quem foi convidado."*
> (To a wedding or baptism only goes who is invited.)
> —Portuguese saying

In general the Portuguese do not easily invite people that are not part of their social circle of close friends and family. But when you are invited to someone's home, you can expect to be treated in a genuinely hospitable manner and be offered food and drink in abundance. The occasion and context of the invitation usually determines the degree of formality. An invitation to a family dinner will be much more informal than a dinner party with colleagues or business partners. If in doubt, ask the host how you should dress. Most Portuguese homes are informal environments, and as long as you are courteous and use common sense, you will not require any special knowledge of etiquette. Depending on the nature of the invitation, it is usually appropriate to bring a gift to a dinner party or informal get-together. This could be flowers or chocolates for the lady of the house, or a bottle of wine, port, or liquor for the male host. In general, the host welcomes arriving guests, takes their coat, jacket, or hat and introduces them to the other guests. A personal introduction may not be possible at a large party or gathering. In this case, it is acceptable for people to introduce themselves.

Breaking the Ice

Even at private social events the Portuguese tend to be reserved at first and mostly talk to those they know. They do not easily socialize with people they have not been introduced to. A formal introduction is thus not merely a formality, but the best and often only way to meet people and make contacts. If you have any contacts in Portugal prior to your arrival, being invited to a social event by them is a perfect opportunity to establish contacts, be they Portuguese or other expatriates.

Dinner Parties

Before sitting down to eat, guests may be offered an aperitif or cocktail. This gives the guests the opportunity to relax over a drink and get to know other guests. Superstition has it that hosts should avoid seating 13 guests around a dinner table. As a sign of good manners men let women sit down first. The host is the first to start eating, and, as a general rule, nobody eats before everyone has been served. Men usually pour the drinks for women. When guests are offered a tray or dish with food, they only serve themselves one helping and do not search for the best pieces. If there is enough food the tray will usually be passed around another time for second servings. A superstition says that saltshakers should not be passed from hand to hand. Instead, they remain on the table and are picked up by the guests as needed. Making noise at the table is a sign of bad manners. This includes clanking with glasses and silverware, smacking, slurping, and burping. People don't talk with food in their mouths. At the end of a meal, it is usually the lady of the house who rises first and gives the signal that the meal is over. Coffee, port, or brandy may be served at the dinner table or in the living room. Dinner guests usually don't leave right after the meal. Instead it is customary to join the other guests a little while longer for conversation. When taking leave from any social event, guests should remember to thank the host for the invitation and the enjoyable food, evening, or event. Out of courtesy and appreciation, it is a good idea to reciprocate a dinner invitation at a later time, although this is not mandatory.

At informal dinners, the meal may be arranged in *jantar-buffet* (dinner buffet) style. This is much more casual than a seated dinner, since the guests can walk around to get food and socialize more freely. The buffet could consist merely of appetizers and drinks, or include a hot entrée that is easy to serve. At a buffet dinner, the host will ask the guests to approach the table where food is served, and the guests help themselves to whatever food they like.

Cocktails and Chá Das Cincos

People have parties for a variety of reasons. This can be a birthday, graduation, engagement, or whatever occasion people decide they want to celebrate. Formal dress is not required at most parties, but people usually dress up. Drinks and snacks are normally provided, but guests often bring a beverage of their choice. The Portuguese are used to staying out late, and since most parties take place on weekends they last until the wee hours of the morning.

A much more formal social event is a cocktail party, known as *beberete* (cocktail), usually with a large number of invited guests. Dress is always formal. Men wear a dark suit and tie or a tuxedo, and women wear a cocktail dress. Cocktail parties are usually early evening events, between six and nine o'clock. In addition to drinks, appetizers and snacks are also served.

Another traditional form of get-together, although generally reserved for ladies is the *chá das cinco* (five o'clock tea). Although this custom is no longer as popular as in the past, which is reflected in the fast disappearance of the once popular teahouses, it is still practiced in some social circles. For such an occasion the lady of the house prepares several kinds of teas, as well as pastries, cookies, and cakes. Although the *chá das cinco* is not a formal event per se, invited guests usually dress neatly.

Making a Visit

Visits to a Portuguese home are mainly reserved for family and intimate friends, and you should not invite yourself unless you are sure that the family's home is open to you. Visits are best announced by telephone. Close friends make unannounced visits to each other's homes, but it is best to avoid arriving at meal times, so you don't give the impression that you are imposing yourself. Personal contacts within the community are very important to the Portuguese, and courtesy visits are made for a variety of reasons. This could be to send birthday greetings, congratulate someone on a birth, visit a sick friend, offer condolences, say farewell, and around Christmas and New Year's, to wish friends and neighbors *boas festas* (happy holidays). The best time for a visit is in the afternoon for coffee or before dinner. If you expect a visitor, it is common to offer coffee or refreshments, and perhaps appetizers, cake, or cookies. As an arriving guest, it is okay to decline food or drink.

Inviting Guests to Your Home

There are many different ways to entertain guests. You could have a Sunday lunch, or afternoon barbecue, a formal seated dinner, a more informal buffet-style meal, or even a cocktail party. When inviting guests to eat, it is important to observe the Portuguese meal times.

Lunch is best served between 1pm and 1:30pm, dinner between 8:30pm and 9:30pm. Arriving guests should be offered a refreshment or alcoholic beverage. Red wine is opened beforehand to breathe, and a bottle of white wine should be served in a wine chiller. Coffee and/ or a digestive usually follow a major meal. In general the occasion and the purpose of the event will determine its formality. The Portuguese dress well to go out, including dinners and parties at someone's home. Unless you clearly specify that an event is informal, expect your guests to dress more on the formal side. As a general guideline, anywhere other than at a party of young people or students, appearances matter and guests will dress up.

APPEARANCES

> *"Bonito por fora, bonito por dentro."*
> (Beautiful on the outside, beautiful on the inside.)
> —Portuguese saying

As the above saying suggests, the Portuguese value appearances, and attire is an important status symbol. A Portuguese friend once told me: "Here in Portugal you could be a vagabond, but as long as you dress well, everyone will treat you as a doctor or lawyer." How people dress is largely dependent on their own status and the status they would like to convey. In fact, anyone who is well dressed receives a certain degree of respect, and someone with a respected title or profession will rarely dress down, not even for leisure activities.

Everyday Attire

Regardless of social class or profession, proper dress is important for most Portuguese. People may be poor, but they will always dress neatly, even though sometimes simply. For everyday work situations dress code is not excessively formal, as long as people dress neatly. Men wear slacks to work and sometimes a blazer, or, if their job requires it, a business suit with tie. Women dress neatly and often quite fashionably and mostly wear only light make-up during the day. Jeans are generally associated with leisure time activities and are only tolerated in more casual work environments. In rural areas fashionable clothing is much less important than in the cities, and for the most part people dress neatly and conservatively. Older people usually dress up to go to town, be it for a doctor's appointment or to go shopping. Leaving one's home and entering the public space demands a certain acceptable appearance in the eyes of the Portuguese, no matter if it is in a city or small village.

As with clothing, it is also important to wear nice shoes. Women seem to pay special attention to elegant footwear, and it is amazing how Portuguese women manage to walk on Portugal's cobbled sidewalks in their stilettos without stumbling. With polished shoes being an important part of people's appearance, it is not coincidental that shoeshine men can still be found in the centers of Portugal's cities, just to shine up those nice shoes before an important meeting or on the way to work.

Dressing for the Occasion

There are many occasions for which the Portuguese dress up. Proper formal attire is reserved for special occasions and important social events such as receptions, banquets, cocktail parties, or balls. Formal dress is not required to go to a concert or the opera, but older people and those who are status-conscious usually dress up for the occasion, while younger ones come in their jeans to listen to Verdi. A tuxedo is worn at cocktail parties, formal dances, galas, and certain receptions. For such elegant occasions women usually wear a cocktail dress or gown. For formal daytime events men usually wear a two or three-piece suit, or for less formal occasions, slacks with a blazer or jacket. Women wear elegant suits or dresses that are not too short nor have a low neckline.

A peculiar habit still common among the older generation is to

*Older Portuguese men tend to dress more
formally in blazers, jackets, and suits.*

dress up on Sundays. This habit probably goes back to the old custom
of putting on your Sunday best for mass. An older couple may just be
enjoying a visit to the local pastry shop or a walk in the park, but they
will both be dressed elegantly on Sundays.

Casual Dressing

About the only time when the Portuguese seem absolutely comfortable
with wearing casual clothing is when they are at the beach or on
vacation. That is the only time where they seem less concerned about
appearance, and where sandals, shorts, and tank tops are common.
But even at restaurants and bars on the esplanades good manners
suggest wearing shorts and a shirt and covering a bathing suit or bikini
with a beach skirt and T-shirt. These rules are less frequently observed
on the Algarve coast and other beach resorts with large numbers of
foreign tourists.

MANNERS AND DEMEANORS

> *"Bom porte com boas maneiras*
> *Abrem portas estrangeiras."*
> (Good conduct and good manners
> Open foreign doors.)
>
> —Portuguese saying

The Importance of Good Manners

Just as a neat appearance, good manners are equally important to the Portuguese, since they are a sign of good education and a respectable social status. Making a good impression and saving face are the main considerations when first meeting someone, and the Portuguese can be polite, although a little stiff and reserved, toward strangers. The Portuguese are known for their *brandos costumes* (mild manners), a gentle, benevolent, non-confrontational, and somewhat submissive attitude. As a result of these mild manners people rarely curse in public. Cursing is considered rude and a sign of low status and education. Similarly, the Portuguese rarely argue or complain. It is more important to avoid a confrontation and not stand out, than defend one's own viewpoint and attract attention. The air conditioning in a long-distance bus may be set at freezing temperatures, but it would take a long time for anybody to complain to the driver. Similarly, parked cars may block sidewalks or building entrances and lines at the post office or bank may snake out the door, but people will gracefully accept these annoyances without complaining. And when they do complain, they do it in such a gentle manner that anyone unfamiliar with the Portuguese mentality is caught off-guard. On several occasions people have pointed out to me in the most friendly and non-confrontational manner that they were ahead of me in a line.

Portugal is a country where traditional values still influence public behavior. Rank, status, and age are important considerations that determine how much respect should be paid to someone in public. As

91

a rule of thumb, younger people get up to offer older ones or pregnant women a seat on a bus. Younger people also give way to older people, and men to women, be it on the street or to enter a building. Since appearances are of great importance, a man in a business suit or with an aura of self-importance can expect to receive more expedient and attentive service almost everywhere.

Privacy and Personal Space

There is little room for physical privacy in a small country such as Portugal. Houses are small, streets are narrow, and stairways are winding. Living together in such close spaces has certainly led to a certain tolerance toward the behavior, noise, and habits of neighbors and passersby. This is probably also why people don't always find it necessary to apologize when inadvertently brushing against each other or when passing at a close distance. In conversation especially, the Portuguese keep much less distance from each other than is customary in Anglo-Saxon cultures. During a conversation, people often tap each other on the arm or shoulder to get the point across, so to speak. They also frequently raise their voice, even when discussing unimportant topics. Neighborhood bars can sometimes get loud with the voices of only a few men discussing a soccer game. Due to space limitations it is customary for guests to share tables at restaurants, especially when no other tables are available. Park benches are shared in a similar manner. On the other hand the Portuguese are very respectful of what I might call mental privacy. They rarely initiate an unsolicited conversation, and seem respectful of one's privacy to the point of appearing shy.

Time

The stressful lifestyle of other modern urban societies has only barely touched this country, and Portugal largely remains a peaceful place with a relaxed pace of life. I met a Spanish couple who had recently moved from Madrid to Lisbon. They had only good things to say about Portugal's sleepy capital. Their main argument was that Lisbon was very laidback in comparison to Madrid's pushy and stressful atmosphere. In fact, one of the most noticeable aspects about Portugal is how much time people have—time for their spouses and children at home, and time for friends at the bar. The Portuguese not only have time for family and friends, but also for many other good things in life. Among them are the lively festivals and dances, as well as the numerous occasions when people get together for meals. It is amazing how much time the Portuguese can spend on social get-togethers. At an outdoor restaurant in Évora a small group of gentlemen in business suits were finishing lunch when I arrived for a coffee mid-afternoon. When I walked past the restaurant after dark, the same gentlemen were still there, drinking wine and talking. Obviously, when it comes to socializing, time stands still in Portugal. Companionship is what matters, not the hours that pass while doing so.

Affection

The Portuguese have no qualms about showing affection in public. Couples hold hands, hug, and kiss in just about any public space without inhibitions whatsoever. Unlike in Anglo-Saxon cultures where affection is reserved for the private sphere, the Portuguese take their affectionate behavior with them to public spaces. This includes their warm relation with their children, as well as with their spouse, boy- or girlfriend. On weekends, all the park benches in Lisbon seem to be occupied by hugging couples as well as families who are all at ease with showing their affection for one other.

Patience

The Portuguese are a patient people, which is probably the best attitude in a country where customer service could use some improvement and where government bureaucracy is overwhelmingly sluggish. For a foreigner, it is difficult to wait in line for half an hour to mail a letter or obtain information without getting infuriated by the inefficiency and slow service, but the Portuguese accept these annoyances with utmost nonchalance. Although slow service is more the rule than the exception, the Portuguese only rarely complain. This attitude can be partly explained by the mild-mannered disposition of the Portuguese, but also in part by their fear to attract undue attention in public.

Ladies First

Call it machismo or the extended age of chivalry, but the relationship between men and women in Portugal is still largely based on traditions that emphasize male prowess and female vulnerability. As a general rule, men treat women in a courteous, considerate, and respectful manner. Very rarely do men whistle at women on the street or otherwise try to attract their attention. Proper manners are what counts in public, and whenever possible men act as gentlemen in front of women. "Ladies first" is still a widely observed rule of Portuguese etiquette, and foreign visitors should be aware of its importance in Portugal's public life. Men hold the doors open for women and help them get in and out of cars. Similarly, men light cigarettes for women, and get up from a chair when a seated woman gets up. A gentleman will also help a lady put on a jacket or a coat. While these courtesies are considered patronizing and largely outmoded in Anglo-Saxon cultures, they still seem to work well in Portugal. Portuguese women seem to appreciate the attention they get from men, and men feel appreciated in their role as gentlemen.

Smoking

Expect little respect or concern for non-smokers in Portugal. People smoke everywhere, even at places with no-smoking signs, such as train compartments. Cafés and bars get especially smoky in the evening hours, and it is quite common for people to smoke at restaurants after a meal. Non-smoking sections at restaurants, bars, cafés, or other public places are unheard of.

Sacred Spaces

The Portuguese are a religious people, and it is important to respect their houses of worship and follow the customary etiquette. When entering a church men take off their hat. Women should cover low-cut necklines and bare shoulders with a scarf. Most Portuguese dip their hand in the receptacle of blessed water near the entrance and make the sign of the cross. This gesture is a reminder of the sacrament of baptism. When passing the tabernacle on the altar, people bend their knees and make a sign of the cross as a sign of faith. Avoid entering a church during mass. This disrupts the service and is a sign of disrespect. I remember visiting the Jerónimos monastery in Lisbon at the time of Sunday mass. Hundreds of tourists, freshly dispatched from their tour buses, crammed through the portal into the main nave of the cathedral, despite the signs posted at the entrance asking visitors to respect the times of worship. The tapping of shoes as people moved from nave to nave, camera flashes, and the noise from conversations all disrupted the devotional atmosphere of the mass and were distracting to worshipers. A busy sightseeing schedule is no excuse for being disrespectful of local customs and religious traditions.

Nudity

The Portuguese are a traditional and conservative people, whose morality is still strongly influenced by the Catholic Church. Topless bars and strip clubs are few and far between and are usually tucked away in hard-to-find corners of Portugal's cities. Nudity is present to a small degree in advertising as well as on some late-night TV shows, but it is largely absent from public life. Topless or nude bathing is not common in Portugal, except on a handful of remote beaches that are mostly frequented by foreign tourists.

— *Chapter Seven* —

A TASTE OF PORTUGAL

"Basta pouco, poucochinho p'ra alegrar,
uma existéncia singela...
É só amor, pão e vinho, e um caldo verde,
verdinho a fumegar na tijela."
(Little is enough, very little,
To give joy to a simple existence...
It is only love, bread and wine, and kale soup,
all green steaming in the bowl.)
   —from the fado *Uma Casa Portuguesa*, sung by
    Amália Rodrigues; lyrics by Reinaldo Ferreira

Although Portugal is a small country, it has a richly varied cuisine.
Every region, and sometimes every town, has its own food specialties,
and the diversity and variety of meat dishes, stews, soups, desserts,
and pastries is truly astounding. Several millennia of experience with

the sea have encouraged a surprising variety of seafood dishes, while Portugal's long tradition of small farmsteads has given rise to a rustic cuisine of meats, such as goat, lamb, rabbit, partridge, and pigeon. Many regional recipes also include locally and seasonally available ingredients which greatly enrich the variety of regional dishes. It is interesting to note however, that despite the historic spice trade with the Orient, Portugal's cuisine today is not known for its spiciness or exotic flavors. Portugal's characteristic dishes are hearty and reveal a traditional skill of creating satisfying and tasty meals with simple ingredients. The spiciest ingredients are onions, garlic, and coriander, one of which is part of almost every recipe. The few spicy dishes with chili peppers and curry that are served on occasion at restaurants are recent introductions by immigrants from former colonies.

THE DAILY FARE

Pequeno Almoço (Breakfast)

Breakfast in Portugal is a quick and light affair. A cup of heated milk or a cup of coffee with a lot of milk, together with *torrada* (buttered toast), is often all the Portuguese eat in the morning. People rarely have breakfast at home during the week and prefer a quick bite at a bakery on their way to work or school. On some occasions or when staying at a hotel, the Portuguese may indulge in a full-course breakfast, which includes a variety of dry cakes, home-made cookies, fruit juices, fresh fruit and fruit preserves, a variety of light cheeses, butter, fresh bread rolls, as well as brioches or croissants.

Almoço (Lunch)

Naturally, after a light breakfast a filling lunch has to follow, and the Portuguese take a long time to enjoy their main meal of the day. At lunchtime most restaurants in city centers cater to the working population by offering cheap and hearty meals. Lunchtime in Portugal is from about noon to 3pm, but restaurants rarely fill up before 1pm. The Portuguese usually eat meat for lunch, and sometimes seafood, accompanied mostly by potatoes. Most meals include only a small serving of vegetables or a small salad. Bread, cheese, and olives accompany most meals, and soup is also fairly common. A good table wine is part of lunch for most Portuguese, and the main course is often followed by dessert, coffee, and, for the diehard, a local brandy known as *bagaço*. Lunch at a Portuguese home is a little simpler and does not necessarily include appetizers, coffee, or dessert, although bread is served with most meals.

Jantar (Dinner)

The dinner menu of the Portuguese is not much different from lunch, except that most people will eat at home, at least during the week. On weekends the Portuguese enjoy going out to dinner, often accompanied by the whole family. Most Portuguese prefer to dine late and dinner is usually served from about 7:30pm to 10pm. On weekends restaurants don't fill up until about 10pm.

EATING IN AND OUT

No matter if you eat at a restaurant or at home, most meals in Portugal are informal and evolve around the simple pleasure of eating. Food is served to fill the belly and to socialize. The social aspect of eating is immensely important. Few people have a meal by themselves. There are usually coworkers, friends, or relatives who share the meal and keep each other company.

Table Etiquette

Portugal's table manners are fairly standard. As long as you use common sense and observe basic rules of etiquette, you will most likely not commit any *faux pas*. The etiquette observed or expected at a restaurant depends on the ambience and the price level. Your first impression of a restaurant will quickly tell you how formal it is. While common restaurants where the Portuguese eat lunch are informal places where sophisticated table manners are not required, a four-star restaurant or an elegant government *pousada* (inn) will require certain knowledge of formal table manners. In rural areas people will doubtlessly bring their rustic manners to the dinner table. The same is true for public events such as picnics and popular festivals, where simpler and more rustic table manners prevail.

Before sitting down to eat, it is a sign of good manners to wash your hands. As a general rule you should not start eating before everyone has been served. Silverware is used from the outside in, that is, if soup is served first, you first take the spoon that is farthest away from the plate. The Portuguese rarely eat with their fingers and when they do, they always use a napkin. Chicken is also eaten with knife and fork, and only very small birds such as partridges are eaten by hand. Fish is not cut with a knife, but with a fork or, at better restaurants, with a fish knife. At the average restaurant it is acceptable to use your hand to take bones or olive pits out of your mouth. Olives and bread are also eaten by hand. Bread is not cut nor eaten whole, but is broken by hand piece by piece as it is eaten. Bread is never used to soak up gravy or clean the plate, at least not at restaurants. Cake is eaten with a dessert fork. Fruit for dessert is usually cut into pieces with a knife and then eaten with the fork. Small fruit such as cherries and grapes are eaten by hand. After finishing your meal put the silverware parallel on the plate, usually with the tip pointing away from you.

Eating at a Restaurant

One of the most pleasant discoveries in Portugal is the fact that there are so few fast-food restaurants. The Portuguese still hold on to the tradition of sitting down and taking their time to eat. No matter where you are in Portugal, there is a restaurant on almost every street corner. Most are simple establishments that serve a standard Portuguese menu with hearty dishes. But with a little bit of searching it is not too difficult to find a slightly more upscale establishment, where eating becomes a more memorable experience.

During the work week you will notice that it is quite common for workers to spend their entire lunch hour at a restaurant. Since restaurants are small, several tables are usually put together, and it is common for strangers to share a table. At lunchtime most people prefer the *prato do dia* or *menu do dia*, the daily special, although restaurants offer a-la-carte meals as well. At most common restaurants the food will be plentiful, but simple. Half portions are often available for those with a lighter appetite. Most restaurants serve bread, butter, cheese, and olives as appetizers, and customers have to pay for what they consume. In some restaurants soup is served after the main course, so make sure you tell the waiter when you want it. *Vinho de casa* (house wine) is very affordable and is served in a *jarro* (ceramic pitcher), often served straight from the cask. Better establishments have a *lista de vinhos* (wine list) for customers to select a bottle of their taste. The traditional guidelines about when to order white or red wine are no longer so strictly observed, but if you like to follow the tradition, here are the guidelines: white wines for fish and poultry, red wines for all other meat. To beckon a waiter (*empregado de mesa*), raise your index finger and say *"faz favor."* Although wait staff in Portugal do not hurry to please a customer or smile continually, most of them are courteous, efficient, and provide good service. The service charge is included in restaurant bills, but it is customary to leave some change as a tip, or more if the service was exceptional.

SUSTENANCE FROM THE SEA

Even before seeking trade routes to the Orient, one of the first reasons for the Portuguese to set out to sea was the search for food. Besides farming, fishing is among Portugal's oldest economic activities. Sardines, cod, haddock, and mackerel have provided a livelihood for coastal Portugal for centuries and continue to play an important role in the national economy. Portugal's waters are also rich with crab, shrimp, squid, octopus, and shellfish, which all find their way into various delicious dishes that are all worth sampling. Seafood is still one of the mainstays of Portuguese cooking today, and it is not surprising to regularly find fish on most restaurant menus and dinner tables, especially along the coast.

Bacalhau—The Faithful Friend

Bacalhau (dried, salted cod) is doubtlessly the food item most associated with Portuguese cuisine. *Bacalhau* is prepared in every possible and imaginable way, from simply grilled, to steamed, cooked in milk, baked, stewed, breaded, and made into fried patties. And even today, in the age of cool houses and refrigerators, *bacalhau* is sold the way it has been for over 500 years: salted and dried. The Portuguese began to catch cod in the North Atlantic most likely even before Columbus reached America. The first fishing fleets left for Greenland,

Dried cod, known as bacalhau, being sold at the weekly market.

Terra Nova (Newfoundland), and Nova Scotia in the late 15th century, and by 1504 the Portuguese had established seasonal fishing colonies in Newfoundland.

Bacalhau is aptly nicknamed *fiel amigo* (faithful friend) by the Portuguese, since it was the staple of Portugal's poor for centuries. During times of famine the city of Lisbon regularly bought shiploads of dried cod from English ships to feed the population. Many popular proverbs refer back to this time, when cod was considered the food of the poor. An old Portuguese saying goes like this:

"Amarelo, salgado, cru e mau
Chama o povo ao bacalhau."
(Yellow, salty, raw, and bad,
Is what people call codfish.)

In contrast to its history as the food of the poor, *bacalhau* is today enjoyed by all Portuguese. In fact, Portugal is among the world's largest consumers of cod, which is mostly imported from Norway, Iceland, Russia, and the U.S.A.

Typical Seafood Dishes

Portugal has an amazing variety of seafood dishes, from simply grilled or fried fish served with potatoes, to rich simmered stews, and shellfish steamed with vegetables. *Arroz de marisco* (seafood rice) is a seasoned stew made with several types of seafood and cooked together with rice. The *caldeirada*, common in Portugal's coastal regions, is another seasoned stew made with a variety of seafood. Very popular is the *caldeirada de mariscos*, a shellfish stew with layers of potatoes and vegetables. *Cataplana* is a traditional dish of steamed seafood from the Algarve. The word *cataplana* means copper pot, and refers to the sealed steaming pan this popular dish is prepared in. Much simpler, but also considered a delicacy are fresh sardines (known as *sardinhas assadas)* grilled on a charcoal grill.

103

HEARTY MEAT DISHES

In addition to the great variety of seafood dishes, Portugal also has a rich selection of meat dishes with great regional variations. Many of these dishes take their origin in the humble kitchens of the rural population, who creatively used a variety of ingredients to make savory dishes from often very simple ingredients. There are bean stews with pig ears and entrails that are carefully seasoned with onions and coriander, and other meats marinated or slowly cooked with vegetables and wine. *Bife à Portuguesa* (sautéed or grilled beef steak topped with a fried egg) is one of the most popular Portuguese beef dishes, while *cozido à Portuguesa* (a stew made with cabbage and meats such as pork, beef, smoked sausage, and chicken) is considered by some to be Portugal's national dish.

While pork and beef are meat items common everywhere, hare, rabbit, partridge, lamb, and kid are especially popular in rural areas, and each region has its own way of preparing them. There is the *chanfana* (lamb stewed in red wine) from the Beiras region, the *cabrito assado com arroz do forno e castanhas* (roasted kid with oven-baked rice and chestnuts) from Trás-os-Montes, and the *ensopado de borrego*, a lamb-stew from the northern Alentejo. The best-known regional dish from Altentejo is *carne de porco à Alentejana* (pork cooked with clams, tomatoes, and coriander), while Porto's most famous dish is the *tripas à moda do Porto* (tripe in Porto style), a stew of beef tripe, sausage, vegetables, and beans. Legend has it that this dish goes back to the preparations for the Portuguese conquest of the Moroccan city of Ceuta in 1415. To supply the ships with enough food for the military expedition, the locals agreed to donate all their good meat, keeping only the entrails for their own consumption.

FAVORITE SOUPS

Soups served in Portugal are rich and hearty, and often a meal by themselves. Quite often they are made from locally available ingredients and reveal the goodness and simplicity of peasant-style cooking of the past. *Açorda*, one of the most characteristic dishes from Alentejo, is a bread soup made from meat, vegetable, or fish stock, and blended with coriander, garlic, olive oil, egg, and more. In a small Alentejo town a local customer at a bar recommended this hardy soup to me in the following way: "*Açorda* is the best soup we have. It gives you a lot of energy, especially after too much drinking, after a festival, or after returning home from a long wake." Another regular favorite on the Portuguese menu is *caldo verde*, a soup of shredded kale, potatoes, and sometimes *chouriço* (smoked sausage). It is simple and delicious and testifies to a long-standing tradition of small vegetable patches that provide the ingredients for *caldo verde* all year round.

OTHER SPECIALTIES

Portugal has a lively cottage industry of homemade specialty foods, and it is worthwhile to try out these local delicacies at regional markets and fairs. Among them are small-production wines, hand-pressed olive oil, pickled olives or other vegetables, handmade cheese and sausages, and smoked meats. Try the *alheiras à Mirandela*, a famous smoked sausage from northern Portugal, made with chicken meat and garlic. Among the many types of cheese, the *queijo da Serra* (from the Serra da Estrela mountains) is probably Portugal's most famous regional cheese. The *amanteigado* variety is mild and buttery, almost liquid, and is eaten by cutting a round hole at the top of the cheese and eating the cheese with a spoon. Other well-known specialty cheeses made from the milk of goats or sheep are the *queijo de Nisa* (Alentejo), the *queijo de Évora* (Alentejo), the *queijo de Castelo Branco* (Beira Baixa), and the *queijo Rabaçal* (Beira Litoral).

PASTRIES

Portugal has a mind-boggling variety of cakes, pastries, and cookies. Most of them go back to the well-kept recipes of Portugal's nunneries, which are today copied and expanded by bakeries everywhere. Every region and almost every town has its special confections, cakes, and pastries that are not available elsewhere. Central Portugal, with its legion of convents and monasteries, has an amazingly rich assortment of baked goods. The nuns' creativity is not only revealed in the diverse ingredients, shapes, frostings, and fillings, but also in the names for these sweet concoctions, which often make humorous references to concepts associated with heaven. Among them are the *barrigas de freira* (nun's bellies), a dessert made of egg yoke, bread, and syrup; *papos de anjo* (angel's cheeks), a type of macaroon; and *toucinho do céu* (heaven's bacon), a confection of egg yokes, almond, and sugar. The following short list is only a sampler of what awaits those with a sweet tooth in pastry shops all over Portugal. Among the best-known regional pastries are the *pastéis de Belém* (custard tarts, a specialty of Lisbon's Belém district), the *queijadas de Sintra* (an almond cheese tart from Sintra, made from cream cheese and a shortbread crust), and *dom rodrigos*, a sweet confectionery from the Algarve, made from eggs, almonds, and sugar, and wrapped in colorful foil. A number of sweet dishes are prepared seasonally for special occasions. Among them are *rabanadas* (made from white bread soaked in sugar syrup, then dipped in beaten eggs and fried), popular in the Minho region at Christmas; *filhós* (a type of fritters), popular in the north around Christmas, and the *folar de Páscoa* (a sweet bread baked with whole eggs inside), popular at Easter.

SNACKS AND APPETIZERS

Sandwiches

There is hardly anything more important for the Portuguese than to sit down and leisurely enjoy a meal. But for those few occasions when there is not much time, there are plenty of snack items sold at bars, cafés, and restaurant counters. Sandwiches (*sande, sanduíche*) are no doubt the most popular snack food and come in a large variety of flavors and ingredients. *Tosta* (toasted sandwiches) are also available everywhere, usually made with ham and cheese (*tosta mixta*). A

*Roasted chestnuts are popular snacks in the
winter and on St. Martin's Day.*

favorite mostly in Porto, is the *Francesinha*, "the little French girl",
a hot sandwich with beef, sausage, and tomato sauce.

Salgados

Salgados (or *salgadinhos*) is the general term for a large variety of
salty appetizers. They are served in bite sizes or in the shape of small
pastries or patties, and usually contain meat, cheese, or seafood.
Popular items found at snack bars are varieties of *pastéis* (pastries)
filled with meat, cheese, or seafood. Other common items are *rissóis*
(deep-fried pastries filled with shrimp, chicken, or meat), *bolinhos de
bacalhau* (fried patties of minced *bacalhau*, pureed potatoes, and
spices), and *empadas* (small pies with fillings such as chicken).

107

Tremoços

Tremoços are lupine seeds, a legume variety, that are pickled and served as free snacks at bars with beer or wine.

ALCOHOLIC BEVERAGES

Alcoholic beverages are an integral part of social life in Portugal. According to statistics, Portugal has one of the highest rates of alcohol consumption in the EU, second only to Luxembourg. Alcohol is indeed a steady companion for many Portuguese, from wine and brandy at lunchtime, to an afternoon beer and evening port after dinner. But whenever people get together and drink, socializing is the main reason for being together. Drinking enhances the atmosphere and puts people in a good mood, but is rarely an aim in itself.

Wine

Wine is Portugal's national beverage and is enjoyed by almost every adult at any time of day. Although internationally not widely known, Portugal's wines are of high quality, and the Portuguese are proud of their 47 different wine-growing regions that produce a large variety of very good wines. The best-known wines are from the following demarcated regions: Minho, Dão, Beiras, Bairrada, Estremadura, Douro, Alentejo, and Ribatejo. The term *reserva* on a label indicates that the wine is produced from an especially selected, excellent harvest. Another mark of quality is D.O.C. (*Denominação de Origem Controlada*, or Appellation of Controlled Origin), the abbreviation of Portugal's appellation system that attests to a wine's designated growing region. A similar seal of quality is VQPRD (*Vinho de Qualidade Producido em Região Demarcada* or Quality Wine Produced in a Demarcated Region). A Portuguese specialty is the so-called *vinho verde* (green wine) from the Minho region. *Vinho verde* is not a wine of green color, but the name refers to the fact that it is a wine made from unripe grapes and with a shorter fermentation period. It is lighter, a tad sparkly, and contains less alcohol (8–9%).

Beer

Although the Portuguese are mostly wine drinkers, there are several large breweries that brew decent beers. Portuguese brews are mostly pilsner-style or lager beers. *Cerveja preta* (dark beer) is also available, but the Portuguese by far prefer the lighter blonde beers. The most popular brands are Sagres, Superbock, Imperial, and Cintra. Imported European beers such as Carlsberg and Heineken are also widely available. Beer on tap is quite popular, and most cafés and bars have at least one beer on tap. Tap beer is known as *cerveja de pressão* or *fino* in some regions, but it is often just called Imperial after Portugal's best draft beer. If you are really thirsty, try a large beer in a mug, a *caneca*.

Port Wine

Port, a fortified wine, is doubtlessly the best-known Portuguese beverage outside of Portugal. Port is enjoyed both as an aperitif before a meal or as dessert wine after a meal. The tradition of crafting port goes back several centuries, and the first recorded shipment of port wine from the mouth of the Douro River was in 1678. The English took a liking to port early on, and the Methuen treaty between England and Portugal in 1703 reduced tariffs on Portuguese wine and English wool, thus making port a more affordable and increasingly popular beverage in England. To protect the purity and quality of port the Marquês de Pombal created the demarcated region of the Douro in 1756, Portugal's first controlled wine growing region. It has remained largely unchanged until today, and no grapes grown outside this area can be used for port.

After the wine harvest the wine is stored in large containers at warehouses near the growing sites on the Douro River, where the primary fermentation takes place and where the grape brandy is blended. In April, before the summer heat can threaten the quality of the wine, the wine is transported to the storehouses in Vila Nova da Gaia, located on the south side of the Douro river, across from Porto.

As the saying goes, *"Os do Douro sabem da vinha, os de Gaia sabem do vinho"* (Those from the Douro region know about the vine, those from Gaia know about the wine.)

There are both red and white varieties of port, but it is the red port that is truly exceptional. There are three main varieties of red port: ruby, tawny, and vintage. Ruby port matures in wooden casks for at least two years, after which it is bottled and sold. Tawny, which means golden reddish brown, refers to ports that are aged in casks for at least six years, but can be aged as long as 30 or 40 years. Tawny port is dryer than ruby, but has added complexity from aging in wooden casks. In years with an exceptional harvest, wineries produce a vintage port. Vintage is the highest quality port. It is aged in oak casks for two to three years and then bottled. The main aging process takes place in the bottle, where the vintage maintains the fruity character of the harvest year and reveals its exceptional flavor over time. Vintage ports age well and can still be consumed after 50 years or more.

Port wine comes in a large variety of brands and prices.

Moscatel

Portugal's muscatel grape variety is only grown in a very small area in the middle Douro valley (around Favaios) and near Setúbal south of Lisbon. It is a sweet liqueur wine of recognized quality with a deep golden color. It is made from grapes that are harvested when very ripe and turned golden by the sun, which gives the wine its characteristic flavor. *Moscatel* contains 18–20% alcohol.

Bagaço

Bagaço is the colloquial name for *aguardente bacageira* or grape brandy. It is made from *bagasse*, the crushed grape husks left over from wine making. *Bagaço* is not aged, which makes it a cheap and somewhat harsh beverage. It is a popular digestive and often consumed after a meal.

Aguardente

This is the general term for Portuguese brandy, distilled from *bagaço*, cereal, or fruits, with an alcohol content of around 40%. The *aguardente velha*, of higher quality, is aged in oak casks for at least two years.

Regional Liqueurs

Portugal is rich in liqueurs of regional fruit. Depending on where you are, you will find liqueur made from a variety of berries and fruits. Especially popular in the Algarve is an almond liqueur called *amêndoa amarga*. The *ginjinha* is a liqueur made from Morello cherries and is popular in Lisbon.

Aguardente de medronho

Commonly known as *medronho*, this spirit is made from the distilled fruits of the strawberry tree, which grows wild in many areas in Portugal. *Medronho* is enjoyed as a digestive and is especially popular in the Algarve. Authentic *medronho* is homemade, but you need to ask around to find it.

COFFEE DRINKS

The Portuguese are veritable coffee addicts, and they drink coffee all day long. Straight espresso, usually taken with a lot of sugar, is the most widely consumed coffee drink in Portugal and is a faithful companion of people's daily activities. No matter how little time people have, there is always time for a shot of espresso at a bar or café counter. Espresso is commonly just called *café* or *café espresso*, but in Lisbon it is mostly known as *bica*. Other coffee drinks include *galão* (milk coffee in a glass), *café com leite* (milk coffee in a cup), *carioca* (watered-down espresso), and *pingado* (espresso with a touch of milk). The *galão* or *café com leite* is the preferred coffee drink in the morning, but after lunch or dinner and at most other times of the day the Portuguese prefer espresso.

Chapter Eight

FOLKLORE AND TRADITION

"*Em Portugal vi eu já*
Em cada casa pandeiro
E gaita em cada palheiro [...]
A cada porta um terreiro
cada aldea dez folias, cada casa atabaqueiro."
(In Portugal already I saw
In every house a tambourine
And a shepherd's flute in every hayloft [...]
At every door a dance ground
In every village ten revelries, in every house a drum
player.)
    —Gil Vicente, from the play *Triunfo do Inverno*, 1529

Portugal is a country rich in folkloric traditions that are still cherished
and practiced everywhere. Each region has its own typical folk tales,

legends, songs, dances, costumes, and handicraft traditions. In a country that is still relatively rural, it is these traditions that bind many communities together and create a sense of identity and belonging.

HANDICRAFTS

Probably more than in any other country in Western Europe, traditional crafts are still widely practiced in Portugal. Every region has its typical handicraft according to long-standing local traditions and everyday needs. Although some of the handmade utilitarian objects are no longer in everyday use, the art of making them is kept alive as part of the regional heritage. The following listing is only a small sampler of Portugal's rich handicraft tradition.

Basket-weaving is still popular.

Cestaria (Basket Weaving)

Basket weaving techniques are still employed to create a variety of utilitarian and decorative objects and the traditions vary greatly from region to region, depending on the various uses and materials. There are sieves for cleaning olives, small baskets for making cottage cheese, and large baskets to harvest grapes, bring produce to the market, or carry fish.

Bordados (Embroidery)

Portugal has a rich embroidery tradition with a large variety of embroidery types that vary from region to region. Cross-stitch, needlepoint, and several other techniques are used to embellish shawls, tablecloths, place mats, napkins, handkerchiefs, night gowns, and blouses.

Rendas (Lacework)

Lacework is produced in a variety of techniques and styles all over Portugal. The *renda de bilro* (Bobbin lace) of Vila do Conde in Minho is among Portugal's best-known lace traditions. The lace is hand-made by using threads wound on bobbins and following a pattern laid out on a pillow.

Tecelagem (Weaving)

Wool, linen, silk, and cotton are commonly used for weaving, and craftspeople have great creative freedom with the materials and the design. Among the best-known weaving traditions are the *capas de honra* (woolen capes) from Trás-os-Montes, the *capote Alentejano* (Alentejo-style cape), and the small rugs from Arraiolos (Alentejo) that are embroidered with cross-stitches, known as *tapete bordado*.

Cerámica (Ceramic)

Portugal has a large number of distinct pottery traditions that all make

115

Traditional ceramics on sale at the weekly Barcelos market.

use of the various types and colors of local clay. Barcelos in northern Portugal is known both for its small, painted clay figurines (mainly the cock of Barcelos, based on a famous legend) as well as for its characteristic red glazed pottery with white dots. Caldas da Rainha, north of Lisbon, is known both for its elegant and artistic pottery as well as figurines. The best-known porcelain in Portugal is the *louça de Coimbra*, the typical blue porcelain from Coimbra with flower and animal motifs.

TRADITIONAL FOLK MUSIC

Portugal's folk music is as diverse as its countryside. Songs revolve around work in the field, harvesting, sowing, as well as important events in one's lifetime such as love and weddings, and also tragedies and funerals. Other songs are work songs of fishermen, market women, bakers, or other professions. Each region has its own traditional dances and songs, which are today preserved by folkloric groups and performed with pride at annual festivals. The most widely used instruments in Portuguese folk music are the *viola* (Spanish guitar) and the *acordeão* (accordion). The concertina, *rabeca* (folk fiddle), and various types of flutes are also widely used. The *gaita-de foles* (bagpipe) is a characteristic component of regional music in northern Portugal. Depending on the type of music and region, there are also several other instruments that are part of folk music ensembles such as the *adufe* (a square-shaped frame drum), the *pífaro* or *fife* (cane flute), and castanets of Spanish origin.

FADO—TUNES FROM THE PORTUGUESE SOUL

> *"O Fado nasceu um dia,*
> *quando o vento mal bulia*
> *e o céu o mar prolongava,*
> *na amurada dum veleiro,*
> *no peito dum marinheiro*
> *que, estando triste, cantava,*
> *que, estando triste, cantava."*
> (The Fado was born one day,
> when the wind hardly stirred
> and the sky lengthened the sea,
> in the rigging of a sailboat,
> in the chest of a sailor
> who, being sad, sang a song,
> who, being sad, sang a song.)
> —from *Fado Português*, lyrics by José Régio, music by
> Alain Oulman

Of all the folkloric music traditions, fado is doubtlessly the music that best expresses the Portuguese sentiments of nostalgia and *saudade*, and it is not coincidental that the melancholic fado tunes have become synonymous with Portugal. The fado, as the name suggests (fado

117

means "fate" in Portuguese), is a ballad about the tribulations of life, about lost loves, about *saudades*, about old friends long lost, and of course also about the feasts, processions, drinking bouts, and other aspects of Lisbon's low life of old. The traditional fado ensemble consists of a *viola-baixo* (acoustic bass guitar), a Spanish guitar, and the twelve-stringed *guitarra Portuguesa* (Portuguese guitar, a long-necked lute). Naturally, the *fadista* (fado singer) is the center of a fado ensemble. It is thanks to her or his voice that the fado develops its peculiar harmonies and mood.

The Roots of Fado

Although the origins of fado are somewhat obscure, it is generally accepted that fado was a dance popular among the Portuguese settlers in 18th century Brazil. When King João VI returned from Brazil in 1821, fado was thus introduced to Portugal. Fado quickly became a popular dance among Lisbon's lower classes, but by 1840 it was mostly performed as a song and no longer as a dance. One of the first famous fado singers was the legendary Maria Severa (1820–1846), a prostitute of Lisbon's Mouraria district. Her musical performances were apparently so captivating that a nobleman, the Count of Marialva, fell head over heels in love with her.

During the first decades of the 20th century, fado gradually became more accepted in higher social circles and began to be performed in Lisbon nightclubs. During the 1930s, numerous fado clubs opened in Lisbon, mostly in the Bairro Alto. Around this time Amália Rodrigues began her career as a fado singer. Thanks to her magnificent voice and soulful interpretations she soon became the undisputed "Queen of Fado" and was somewhat of a cultural ambassador for Portugal during the Salazar years by making fado known around the world. During the *Estado Novo* the fado tunes were predominantly romantic, excessively nostalgic, and they always glamorized Portugal. After the 1974 revolution, fado was shunned for a number of years as it reminded too many people of the dictatorship.

The Fado of Coimbra

A distinct fado tradition began to develop in the city of Coimbra between 1870 and 1880, when students from Lisbon introduced the fado there. Coimbra's fados are nostalgic ballads about the loves and lives of university students sung by groups of male students. Although the fado tradition of Coimbra may seem anachronistic at times, with groups of men in their traditional black university outfits, the Coimbra fado continues to be renewed by successive generations of students, who enter the university and perform the music that glorifies student life, music, and love.

Fado Live and Alive

Although fado today is often performed for tourists in so-called fado clubs, there are also numerous *tascas*, small taverns in Lisbon's Alfama and Bairro Alto districts, where the locals crowd together to sing fado for each other, over a glass of watered-down wine and much sentiment of *saudade*. There is a surprisingly large number of young people that crowd into the *tascas* to hear fado, which is a sure sign that fado has succeeded in bridging the generation gap and also appeals to younger people. This is certainly in part thanks to a young generation of charismatic fado singers that has come of age since the death of Amália Rodrigues in 1999. Many of these young talents do not shy away from experimenting with new forms of expression and taking the fado a little bit beyond its traditional boundaries. Among the young and talented fado stars are Marisa, Mísia, Christina Branco, Katia Guerreiro, Mafalda Arnauth, Teresa Tapadas, Marta Dias, and Ana Sofia Varela. Camané stands out as one of the few male singers among the new generation of fado singers.

FOLKLORIC DANCES

Folk dances are performed at all kinds of festivals all over Portugal, from pilgrimages to religious festivals and of course the lively celebrations of the *santos populares* (popular saints) in June. Much of

119

*Folkloric groups are often dressed in
traditional regional attire.*

Portugal's traditional dances are today performed by folkloric ensembles known as *ranchos folclóricos*. These groups are often made up of men and women of all ages from one village or town, who get together regularly to rehearse the songs and dances. Among Portugal's most popular and characteristic folk dances are the *bailarico* (popular in the Estremadura region), the *chula* (a challenge song home to the Minho and Douro region), the *vira* (a rural waltz typical of northern Portugal), and the *fandango* (a popular dance with fast footwork and heel tapping). The *dança dos pauliteiros* is a fast-paced stick dance performed only by select folkloric groups of men. It is somewhat similar to the English Morris dance, with a complex choreography in which sticks are beaten against one other. In addition to folk music and dances, the regional costumes also form an integral part of folkloric performances. The traditional costumes worn are often those traditionally worn during pilgrimages or at Sunday mass.

FESTIVALS, FAIRS, AND PILGRIMAGES

"Duas Noites há no ano
Que alegram o coração
É a noite de natal
E a noite de São João."
(Two nights during the year
Rejoice the heart.
It is the night of Christmas
And the night of Saint John.)

—Portuguese proverb

Portugal is rich in festivals, and the busy festival calendar extends throughout the year. In addition to the official national and Catholic holidays, there are many religious holidays and festivals that are observed regionally. Almost every village and town has its own festival in honor of its patron saints (*festa de santo patroeiro* or *festa de orago*) in addition to lively fairs and other celebrations. These regional festivities are found all over Portugal and are rich in folkloric traditions with processions, dances, folk music, agricultural shows, and bullfights. If interested in a detailed calendar of local events, contact the respective region's tourist office or, for an overview, buy one of the several *almanaques* (almanacs) such as *Borda d'Agua* or *O Seringador*, available at newsstands. Below I have listed the most important and best-known of these festivals, fairs, and pilgrimages.

121

January

Dia dos Reis or Adoração dos Magos (Epiphany)

Groups of singers dress up as kings and wander from house to house asking for charitable donations. There are several regional variations to this old Catholic tradition. In Portugal, Epiphany is celebrated on the Sunday that falls between January 2 and 8.

February

Dia de São Valentim or Dia dos Namorados (St. Valentine's Day or Day of Lovers)

On St. Valentine's Day, celebrated on February 14 all over Portugal, lovers give each other tokens of their love, such as flowers or small presents. In some regions young women give their lovers a *lenço de namorados* or "lovers' handkerchief", which is embroidered with flowers, heart motifs, and love verses.

Carnaval (Mardi Gras)

Carnaval takes place on the four days before Ash Wednesday. It is celebrated all over Portugal, and traditions vary from town to town. The best known and liveliest carnaval festivities are held in Estoril (near Lisbon), Montijo (near Lisbon), Nazaré (Estremadura), Torres Vedras (Estremadura), Sesimbra (near Setúbal), Sines (Alentejo), Loulé (Algarve), and Portimão (Algarve).

March/April

Festa de Semana Santa (Holy Week Festival)

Easter is the most important religious festival in Braga in the Minho region and is doubtlessly the most lavish Easter celebration in all of Portugal, with numerous processions throughout Holy Week.

Nossa Senhora da Saúde (Our Lady of Good Health)

This large annual procession is held on April 20 in honor of Our Lady of Good Health in Lisbon's Mouraria and Martim Moniz neighborhoods. The procession was initiated in 1570 to ask for protection against the plague.

May

Festas do Santo Cristo (Santo Cristo Festivities)

This is the largest festival in Ponta Delgada in the Azores, in honor of Christ, whose gilded image has been venerated for centuries for its miraculous qualities.

Nossa Senhora de Fátima (Our Lady of Fátima)

May marks the beginning of the pilgrimage cycle that takes place every 12th and 13th day of the month from May to October in Fátima, in remembrance of the six apparitions of the Virgin Mary in 1917.

123

Festa da Queima das Fitas (Burning of the Ribbons)
A student feast in Coimbra, held during the first half of May to celebrate the end of the academic year. Students hold a long procession and burn the ribbons of their academic department.

June

Festa de São Gonçalo (St. Gonçalo Festival)
Celebrated in Amarante in the Douro region, this is a popular feast of the town's patron saint, who is also a patron saint of lovers. Touching São Gonçalo's tomb is supposed to help young people find a marriage partner. During this festival, based on an ancient pagan ritual, lovers give each other erotic pastries in the shape of a phallus.

Festa de Santo António (Festival of St. Anthony)
One of Portugal's most popular and lively festivals. It is held from June 14–29 in Lisbon in honor of Portugal's secondary patron saint. Folkloric groups of the different districts parade through the streets, accompanied by music. This festival is also held in several other towns in central Portugal, mostly on June 13, which is the actual saint's day.

Festa de São João (Festival of St. John)
This festival is held in Porto on June 23 and 24 in honor of St. John, the city's patron saint. The huge festival attracts enormous crowds every year, with music and dance all night long. This festival is also very popular in Braga (Minho), Vila do Conde (Minho), Evora (Alentejo), and Figueira da Foz (Douro).

July

Festival do Colete Encarnado (Festival of the Red Vest)
This popular festival, held during the first week of July in Vila France de Xira (Ribatejo), includes music, dance, and running of bulls.

Festival dos Tabuleiros (Tabuleiros Festival)
This is one of the most colorful festivals in Portugal, held every four years at the beginning of July in honor of the Holy Spirit. The highlight of the festival, held in Tomar in Ribatejo, is a long procession of several hundred women in white costumes wearing large headdresses called *tabuleiros*. The procession moves around town through richly decorated streets.

Festa da Ria (Estuary Festival)
This is a large festival in Aveiro (Beira Litoral) with folk dances and a competition for the most beautifully decorated *barcos moliceiros*, the traditional boats used to collect seaweed for use as fertilizer.

August

Festas Gualterianas (St. Walter Festival)
This is a popular festival in honor of St. Walter, held on the first Sunday in August in Guimarães in the Minho region, with a carnival, fair, processions, and bullfights.

Festa da Senhora da Boa Viagem (Festival of Our Lady of a Safe Journey)
Held on the first weekend in August in Peniche in Estremadura, this festival includes a maritime procession, during which the statue of the saint arrives in the harbor by boat and is then taken on a procession around town.

Nossa Senhora da Agonia (Our Lady of Sorrows)

Held on the weekend closest to August 20, this important religious festival includes folkloric performances, bullfights, and a colorful procession of farmers and fishermen who come into town with ox carts for a festive blessing. It is celebrated in the town of Viana do Castelo (Minho).

Festa do Senhor do Calvário (Festival of the Lord of the Calvary)

Held on the second Sunday in Gouveia (Beira Alta) in August, this is the largest pilgrimage of central Portugal, with processions, fireworks, and lively festivities.

September

Nossa Senhora dos Remédios

A very large festival and pilgrimage held from September 6 to 8 at the famous Baroque sanctuary in Lamego (Douro), with several processions, a fair, music, dance, and other attractions.

Festa do Avante (Avante Festival)

Portugal's largest music and cultural festival takes place in Seixal, near Lisbon. It is held during the first weekend in September and has been organized annually since 1976 by Portugal's Communist Party.

October

Feira de Outubro (October Fair)

A great fair in Vila Franca de Xira with bull runs through town and bullfights in the arena.

Nossa Senhora de Fátima (Our Lady of Fátima)
The last great pilgrimage of the year takes place from October 12–13, with masses and candlelight processions at night.

November/December

Dia dos Fiéis Defuntos (All Souls' Day)
On November 2, people all over Portugal pray for the dead and visit the graves of loved ones.

Feira Nacional do Cavalo (National Horse Fair)
This large horse show in early November coincides with the Feira de São Martinho (St. Martin's Fair) held during the week before St. Martin's day on November 11. The festival, which takes place in Golegã (Ribatejo), includes horse shows and running of bulls.

Dia de São Martinho, St. Martin's Day
Although not an official holiday, St. Martin's Day on November 11 is celebrated all over Portugal. This is the time of year to get together with friends to taste the new wine and eat freshly roasted chestnuts. As the saying goes: "*No dia de São Martinho, vai na adega e prova o vinho*" (On St. Martin's Day go to the wine cellar and try the wine).

São Silvestre (St. Sylvester Festival)
Funchal on Madeira Island is known for its lively St. Sylvester Festival, which falls on New Year's Eve. Festivities usually culminate in a great firework display.

127

— Chapter Nine —

TOUCHED BY THE MUSES

"*E aqueles que por obras valerosas*
Se vão da lei da Morte libertando
—Cantando espalharei por toda parte,
Se a tanto me ajudar o engenho e arte."
(And those who free themselves
Through valuable works from the law of death
—I will make known everywhere in singing,
If ingeniousness and art will help me to such end.)
　　　　　—Luis de Camões, *Os Lusíadas*, Canto I, verse 2

LITERATURE

The Age of Chivalry
The first literary genre to develop in the Portuguese language was the

medieval minstrel song of the 12th century. It was during this early period of literary production that the Portuguese developed a penchant for lyrical and love poetry, which has shaped Portuguese literature for centuries and still remains a strong influence in poetry and song. The troubadour tradition had its climax under King Afonso III (1248–1279). His son, Dinís, (1279–1325) was an enthusiastic patron of music and literature, and was himself a prolific troubadour. During the 15th century Portuguese literature became more diverse. The *romanceiros* (ballads of chivalry, war, and adventure) replaced the minstrel song as the most popular form of literary expression, and in 1434, King Duarte appointed Fernão Lopes as the royal chronicler. He thus gave an initial impulse to historical writing, which would become one of the country's most characteristic literary traditions.

The Golden Age and Beyond

Starting in the early 16th century Renaissance influences began to spread to Portugal. Gil Vicente (1465–1536) was the greatest playwright of his time and is considered the founder of classical Portuguese theater. He wrote 44 farces, comedies, and dramas, and often made fun of social conventions and criticized the religious and secular powers.

Without any doubt, Luís de Camões (1525–1580) was Portugal's most important literary figure of all time. Camões was a poet, soldier, and adventurer, who was banned from court, exiled in Morocco, and spent almost twenty years in India. Camões never became rich on his adventures, but he succeeded in enriching his country with his unrivaled *Os Lusíadas* (The Lusiads, 1572), an epic poem in the classical tradition about Vasco da Gama's voyage to India. Camões' epic raised the Portuguese discoveries to the level of epic grandeur and gave a strong sense of identity to the Portuguese nation as well as a sense of pride in its historic accomplishments. The poetic power of his work remains alive until this day, including his many love poems.

Spanish control of Portugal from 1580 to 1640 brought an end to

Portugal's Golden Age, the country's most prolific era of artistic and literary production. Few notable works of literature were produced until the great revival of Portuguese literature during the 19th century.

The 19th Century

During the 19th century all literary genres experienced a remarkable revival carried out by a large number of talented writers, poets, and historians. Early on in the 19th century Portuguese writers began to absorb the influences of the Romantic movement from abroad. The most notable writers of this period were João Baptista de Almeida Garrett (1799–1854), an accomplished poet and dramatist, and Alexandre Herculano (1810–1877), a respected historian and ethnographer. The foremost 19th century romantic novelists were António Feliciano de Castilho (1800–1875) and Camilo Castelo Branco (1825–1890). In the second half of the 19th century, modern influences such as Realism began to spread among young writers. Eça de Queirós (1845–1900) is considered the most accomplished Realist novelist of the 19th century, and his work profoundly influenced Portuguese literature. Among his best-known novels are *O Crime do Padre Amaro* (The Crime of Father Amaro, his first novel, 1876), and *Os Maias* (The Maias, 1888), a chronicle of several generations of a Lisbon upper class family.

The Road to Modernity

Without any doubt, Fernando Pessoa (1888–1935) was Portugal's most important modern poet. Although hardly known during his lifetime, his posthumously published works of poetry had a profound influence on Portuguese literature and the arts. He was part of the modernist movement that loosely united several other Portuguese poets of the time, among them Mário de Sá Carneiro. Only one book of poems was published during his lifetime (titled *Mensagem*), although he wrote for several literary magazines. Pessoa wrote poetry under several pseudonyms, among them Alberto Caeiro, Ricardo

Reis, Alvaro de Campos, and Bernardo Soares, through which he expressed different world views, sensitivities, and personality traits.

Other important literary figures of the early 20th century were the novelists Aquilino Ribeiro (1885–1963) and José Régio (1901–1969), as well as Miguel Torga (1907–1995). The 1960s were characterized by young poets who revolted against the stifling atmosphere of the dictatorial regime, either through political poetry or attempts to broaden the aesthetic language and artistic norms of the time.

Beyond the 1974 Revolution

With the end of censorship after the 1974 revolution, Portuguese novelists and poets began to explore political themes that had been prohibited for decades. Literary works dealt with the authoritarianism and brutality of the military regime, as intellectuals tried to come to terms with over four decades of stifled creativity and censorship. It was in the years following the revolution that José Saramago (born 1922) emerged as a novelist. His novels not only deal with the social, historical, and political reality of his home country, but also indulge in philosophical musings about human nature, love, power, and other eternal themes. In 1998, Saramago became the first writer of the Portuguese language to be awarded a Nobel Prize in literature. His best-known novels are *Memorial do Convento* (Baltasar and Blimunda, 1982), *O Evangelho Segundo Jesus Cristo* (The Gospel According to Jesus Christ, 1991), and *Ensaio Sobre a Cegueira* (Blindness, 1995).

Although Saramago remains the most visible representative of 20th century Portuguese literature, he is certainly not the only one worth reading. José Cardoso Pires (1925–1998) was a distinguished novelist, know for works such as *O Hóspede de Job* (Job's Guest, 1963) and *Balada da Praia dos Cães* (Ballad of the Beach of the Dogs, 1983). Another influential modern writer is Agustina Bessa-Luís (born 1922) with novels such as *A Sibila* (The Sibyl, 1954) and *Fanny Owen* (1979). António Lobo Antunes is among Portugal's most experimental writers, with a style resembling stream of consciousness.

In his books he explores the internal lives of people shattered by the colonial wars and their experiences in Africa. Among his best-known works are *Fado Alexandrino* and *A Ordem Natural das Coisas* (The Natural Order of Things). Other established contemporary writers whose work is noteworthy are Lídia Jorge, Mário de Carvalho, Almeida Faria, Hélia Correia, and Mário Cláudio.

MUSIC

> *"Quem canta, o mal espanta."*
> (Who sings, scares evil away.)
>
> —Portuguese saying

The Classical Tradition

Although Portugal is not known for its classical music, the country has a long and outstanding tradition of musical production. The first notable works of musical creation in Portugal were the minstrel songs of the troubadours, which became widely popular around the time of Portugal's independence. Several Portuguese kings were accomplished troubadours and many of their songs and lyrics have been preserved to this day. Among the most accomplished troubadours were the Portuguese kings Sancho I, Afonso III, and Dinís. Much of the music written in Portugal over the century was religious music, and sacral compositions remained a strong tradition for many centuries. Carlos Seixas (1704–1742) was Portugal's most accomplished Baroque composer. He wrote over 100 sonatas for keyboard, in addition to religious and orchestral music. João Domingos Bomtempo (1775–1842) was the first Portuguese composer to write symphonies. Alfredo Keil (1850–1907) is probably Portugal's best-known classical composer. Keil is mostly known as the composer of Portugal's national anthem *A Portuguesa*, but he also wrote numerous symphonic pieces and three operas. *Serrana* (1899), a tragic love story from the Serra da Estrela mountains, is his best-known opera.

Among the best-known composers of the early 20th century are Fernando Lopes-Graça (1906–1995), who included folkloric influences in many compositions, and Cláudio Carneyro (1895–1963), best known for his chamber music. Other noteworthy modern composers are Armando José Fernandes (1906–1983), Jorge Croner de Vasconcelos (1910–1974), and Joly Braga Santos (1924–1988). Braga Santos wrote symphonies and several operas and also experimented with challenging musical forms such as chromaticism and atonality. Most of the classical music pieces performed in Portugal today are compositions by international composers, but cultural institutions occasionally also perform the works of great Portuguese composers from the past and present.

Popular Music

Since freedom of speech was seriously curtailed during the dictatorship years, artists and musicians sought other ways of expressing their sentiments and opinions. Especially during the 1960s political and protest songs became a popular way of spreading political messages and expressing discontent. One of the most enigmatic songwriters of this period was José Afonso (1929–1987), known as Zeca Afonso. On the eve of April 25, 1974, Afonso's protest song of brotherhood and equality, *Grândola Vila Morena* (banned after it was first released in 1971), was broadcast to give the signal for the revolt of left-leaning officers against the dictatorship. Other songwriters whose songs often have political content are Sérgio Godinho, Fausto, and Vitorino. Little known abroad, but much respected in Portugal is Carlos Paredes, the undisputed master of the *guitarra Portuguesa*.

Contemporary Trends

For a small country Portugal has a very diverse and active music scene. From traditional folk music to the somewhat vulgar *música pimba* (often with lyrics containing sexual references and bad language) and the stars of Portugal's pop scene, Portugal's music has something to offer to every musical taste. Contemporary popular music can be mostly characterized as a fusion of ballads and modern rhythms. Musicians only rarely move into styles such as punk or hard rock. Most tunes are gentle and lyrical, as if the Portuguese were incapable of expressing anger or negative sentiments in their music or lyrics. Among the best-known stars of the national music scene are the singers and songwriters Luís Represas, Rui Veloso, Jorge Palma, and the well-established rock/pop bands Xutos e Pontapés, Delfins, and Ala dos Namorados. Other well-known bands that combine international styles with Portuguese elements are Vozes da Rádio, Santos e Pecadores, Macaus, and Repórter Estrábico. The best-known female performers are Mafalda Veiga, Né Ladeiras, Susana Felix, and Dulce Pontes.

Given Portugal's vast folkloric musical tradition it is not surprising that contemporary music continues to draw from traditional roots. There are several groups that take their inspiration from Portugal's

A traditional folk music ensemble.

folk music while experimenting with new forms of musical expressions. Among them is the accordion quartet Dança Oculta, and the bagpipe and percussion ensemble Gaiteiros de Lisboa. The creative duo of Maria João and Mário Laginha is another one of Portugal's great ensembles that fuse a variety of different musical traditions, in this case jazz and folkloric Portuguese elements. The best-known Portuguese band whose songs are influenced by Portugal's folkloric traditions is Madredeus, a group based on the magical voice of Teresa Salgueiro and the song-writing talent of Pedro Ayres de Magalhães. Their lyrical and poetic ballads with their characteristic melancholic mood have captured audiences around the world.

ART AND ARCHITECTURE

Ancient Beginnings
The first works of art in Portugal were carved and painted horses,

aurochs, and mountain goats created by hunting tribes during the upper Paleolithic period between 25,000 and 18,000 B.C. In the first millennium B.C., the migrating Celts brought with them advanced artistic skills in stone carving, jewelry making, and pottery, with many magnificent examples found mostly in northern Portugal. The Roman occupation of Portugal gave rise to a completely new period of artistic activity. Several excellent examples of Roman mosaics, sculptures, and funerary steles remain from this time. In Évora, in the Alentejo province, are the remains of the largest Roman temple on the Iberian Peninsula. The Visigothic presence that followed the long Roman presence left few artistic and architectural traces, except the remains of a few small 7th century churches with murals. It is also interesting to note how little artistic evidence is left from over 400 years of Moorish presence in Portugal.

Romanesque and Gothic Art

A period of construction and expansion followed the Christian reconquest of the Portuguese territory, and the first monumental structures in the young kingdom were the large Romanesque cathedrals in Braga, Porto, Coimbra, Lisbon, and Évora. Starting in the late 12th century, Gothic art and architecture spread to Portugal. The earliest example is the Cistercian monastery at Alcobaça (begun in 1178), which also houses the tombs of Pedro I and his beloved wife Inês de Castro (ca. 1360), among the most outstanding examples of medieval sculpture. Another noteworthy example of Gothic architecture is the Batalha monastery (begun in 1386), commissioned by King João I after the victory in the battle of Aljubarrota.

The Manueline Style and the Renaissance

The early 16th century saw for the first time an artistic development that was uniquely Portuguese and reflected the country's newly found wealth from overseas trade. After the voyage of Vasco da Gama, Manuel I commissioned several large buildings, in a late or flamboyant

Gothic style that is now known as the Manueline style. Inspired by the Portuguese maritime discoveries, buildings were adorned with motifs from seafaring, such as armillary spheres, corals, seaweed, ship hulls, and sea monsters. Moorish decorative elements were also incorporated into the new style.

The most magnificent examples of Manueline architecture and sculpture are the Jerónimos monastery and the Tower of Belém in Lisbon, the incomplete chapels at the Batalha cathedral, and the magnificent Abbey at the Convent of Christ in Tomar.

The Portuguese Baroque

After a period of the rational and austere style of Mannerism, Baroque influences became noticeable in Portuguese art and architecture in the mid-17th century. The best examples of early Portuguese Baroque are Santa Engrácia in Lisbon (begun in 1682), now the Panteão Nacional (National Pantheon), and Bom Jesus da Cruz in Barcelos (1701–1704), both built by architect João Antunes. The most magnificent

The Belém Tower, one of the great buildings of the Age of Discovery.

example of Portuguese Baroque dates from the reign of João V (1706–1750). To pay a vow for the birth of his first child, João V commissioned the German architect Ludovice to design the palace convent at Mafra. Built from 1717 to 1730, this extravagant Baroque palace displays the best and most precious materials available at the time. Among the most characteristic elements of Portuguese Baroque are the richly gilded wood carvings, known as *talha dourada*. Baroque flourished when the gold from Brazil was plentiful, and this wealth is reflected in the lavish gilded decorations of many churches built at the time. The last great accomplishment of Portuguese Baroque architecture was Bom Jesus do Monte near Braga, built by architect Carlos Luís Ferreira Amarante from 1784 to 1811. It is not just a church, but an entire mountainside transformed into a sanctuary with winding double staircases and chapels depicting the Passion of Christ.

Neoclassicism and the 19th century

The 1755 Lisbon earthquake brought down in a few minutes what had taken Portuguese kings and architects hundreds of years to build. Marquês de Pombal, the minister of state under King José I, took it upon himself to rebuild Lisbon by employing the latest ideas of urban planning and neoclassical design.

The abolition of religious orders in 1834 ended the predominance of religious art in Portugal. In 1836, fine arts academies in Lisbon and Porto opened their doors and began to spread neoclassical influences in the visual arts. In the second half of the 19th century artists began to take interest in naturalism and realism, as well as romantic currents in art.

Modernism and Beyond

Naturalism remained the dominant style in Portuguese art until after the turn of the century, when Portuguese painters gradually began to take interest in contemporary international trends. José de Almada Negreiros (1893–1970) was one of the most diverse artists of the Modernist period. His work includes illustration, design, painting, as well as large-scale mural projects. Among Portugal's most famous modern painters is Maria Helena Vieira da Silva (1908–1992), who spent most of her life in France and developed a semi-abstract style based on landscapes and cityscapes. Lourdes Castro (b. 1930) stands out as one of the most prolific artists of her generation. She worked in lyrical abstraction and later in a variety of experimental genres. Among the most important artists that emerged during the 1960s and 1970s are Fernando Calhau (b.1948), António Palolo (b.1946), Eduardo Batarda (b.1943), as well as the female painters Graça Morais (b.1948) and Ilda David (b.1950). In addition to the traditional media of painting and sculpture, numerous contemporary artists work in experimental media, such as installations, mixed media, video and photography, among them Carlos Nogueira and Julião Sarmento. José Guimarães is among Portugal's best-known contemporary sculptors, and several of his large colorful pieces are displayed in public places in Lisbon and elsewhere.

After the end of the military regime in 1974, international styles in art and architecture became more accepted in Portugal. The Museu Serralves in Porto is among the most outstanding architectural examples of the 1980s. It was designed by Alvaro Siza Vieira, who is one of Portugal's best internationally known architects. The Centro Cultural de Belém, designed by Vittorio Gregotti and Manuel Salgado and completed in 1992, combines the look of a medieval castle with post-modern design. The Parque das Nações is perhaps the most eclectic example of Portuguese architecture of the late 20th century. Home to the 1998 World Expo, the permanent structures were designed by several different architects and show a variety of concepts and styles. Among the most interesting examples is no doubt the Pavilhão Atlântico (designed by Portuguese architect Regino Cruz), a multi-purpose performance hall, whose shape resembles a horseshoe crab.

The Contemporary Scene

Portugal's contemporary art scene is mainly centered in Porto and

Lisbon. Porto's Museu Serralves often shows works of contemporary artists, many of them Portuguese. The Porto art gallery scene is concentrated on Rua Miguel Bombarda, and the monthly opening receptions form a vital part of the local cultural life. In Lisbon several institutions such as the Gulbenkian Foundation (a bequest by Armenian oil magnate Calouste Gulbenkian), Culturgest (a cultural organization owned by Portugal's largest bank Caixa Geral de Depósitos), and the Museu do Chiado regularly have exhibitions of upcoming and established contemporary artists in a broad variety of styles and techniques, from photography to installation and video art. In Lisbon, 15 galleries all over the city participate in the bimonthly LisboArte Contemporânea, a simultaneous showing of contemporary art, with opening receptions on weekends.

AZULEJOS

One of the most characteristic elements of Portuguese architecture and decorative arts are the glazed tiles known as *azulejos* (pronounced "ah-zoo-LAY-shos"). The most magnificent examples can be found in churches, monasteries, and palaces, but they also adorn the façades of old commercial and apartment buildings. Although *azulejos* are today considered a uniquely Portuguese decorative art form, they were originally introduced to Portugal from Moorish Spain at the beginning of the 16th century. Portuguese workshops soon began to take up tile making, and developed a unique tradition of their own. Portugal is today best known for its blue tile designs, a technique of Dutch origin. Portuguese *azulejos* have become so much associated with the color blue (*azul*) that it is often erroneously assumed that the word *azulejo* comes from *azul*. The term *azulejos,* however, is derived from the Arabic word *al zulaïque*, which means smooth and polished stone.

In the late 19th and early 20th century, an increasing number of ceramic artists and painters began to work with *azulejos* and introduced new stylistic elements from Modernism, art nouveau, and later from

An 18th century azulejo motif.

abstract art. The painter Maria Keil was one of the first artists to use modern *azulejo* designs in an urban context. From 1959 to 1972 she designed several *azulejo* panels for the Lisbon subway, combining traditional pattern motifs and subject matter with modern design elements. In fact, the Lisbon subway has become the most prominent outlet for Portuguese artists working with *azulejos*, often with surprisingly modern and experimental designs. Thanks to the adaptability of *azulejos* to diverse techniques and designs, glazed tiles continue to play a vital role in the decoration of public buildings and spaces today. One of the most recent and interesting examples is the Parque das Nações, where several Portuguese artists created *azulejo* panels for the 1998 World Expo.

PORTUGUESE CINEMA

Cinema is not as vital an art form in Portugal as music, literature, or poetry. But although Portuguese films have never been box office hits and are not well-known internationally, there are some very remarkable productions that certainly match up to films made elsewhere in Europe. Portuguese films also have a regular and successful presence at European film festivals, where Portuguese directors have won numerous prizes.

An Overview of Portuguese Cinema

In 1896, a photographer from Porto made a series of short films of regional interest. The presentation was successful and soon movie theaters began to open in Porto and Lisbon. Film productions during the silent era were diverse, but dramatic elements with regional or national subject matter were predominant. One of the classics of Portuguese silent cinema is *Maria do Mar* (1930) by Leitão de Barros, a drama about the lives of fishermen. Barros continued to make successful sound movies, many of which were popular during their time and are today considered classics of Portuguese cinema. The movies of fado singer Amália Rodrigues from the 1940s and 1950s are also worth seeing, at least for their great fado tunes, among them *Capas Negras* (1947) and *Fado, História d'uma Cantadeira* (1947). At the beginning of the 1960s, young directors, who had studied abroad, began to make films that reflected the daily reality of the Portuguese people without the romanticism and nationalism so common at the time. *Os Verdes Anos* (1963) by Paulo Rocha, a drama about young love in a Lisbon suburb, and *Belarmino* (1964) by Fernando Lopes, a semi-documentary about a boxer of humble background, were the most enigmatic works of a generation tired of comedies and historical dramas. These filmmakers loosely formed a movement known as *Cinema Novo*, or "New Cinema," which was committed to realism in film.

Manoel de Oliveira

Portugal's best-known director is doubtlessly Manoel de Oliveira, born in 1908, one of Europe's most enigmatic filmmakers. In his long career he made over 40 movies, many of which have received international awards. His style is fluid, philosophical, and neither storyline nor plot dominates his films, which often indulge in philosophical musings about God, good and evil, destiny, and the virtues and vices of human behavior. Among his best-known recent movies are *O Convento* (The Convent, 1995), starring John Malkovich and Catherine Deneuve; *Viagem ao Princípio do Mundo* (Voyage to the Beginning of the World, 1997); and *A Carta* (The Letter, 1999).

Contemporary Currents

While Oliveira's films are certainly Portugal's greatest contribution to the seventh art, the younger generation of filmmakers also attracts attention with interesting and experimental movies. Among them are João César Monteiro (1939–2003), António Reis, Margarida Cordeiro, Lionel de Oliveira, José Fonseca e Costa, João Mário Grilo, João Botelho, Jorge Silva Melo, Seixas Santos, Pedro Costa, and several others. Subject matter is very diverse, from psychological dramas to adventures and stories about Portugal's recent past. Many Portuguese movies are based on the works of Portugal's great literary figures, which often gives the films an erudite and literary quality.

Chapter Ten

SOCIALIZING AND RECREATION

"Oiça lá ó Senhor Vinho
Vai responder-me mas com franqueza
Porque é que tira toda a firmeza
A quem encontra no seu caminho?"
(Listen up, Mister Wine
Answer me, but with frankness
How come you take all firmness
From those you meet on your way?)
—from *Oiça lá ó Senhor Vinho,* written by Alberto Janes

FAVORITE PASTIMES

The Portuguese are a sociable people, and most recreational activities take place in the company of others. The Portuguese love to gather with neighbors for a game of cards or dominoes, with friends at a bar for a drink, and enthusiastically attend folkloric festivals and dances. Although social activities within the community are important, the Portuguese are family-oriented people and spend most of their spare time with close family and relatives. On weekends, families visit restaurants, shopping centers, and beaches and gather for picnics in parks or nature areas outside town.

A Country by the Beach

With a coastline of nearly 1,800 km (1,118 miles), it is not surprising that beaches are an important leisure destination for the Portuguese. Every weekend during the summer large crowds descend on Portugal's beautiful beaches in search of their own spot in the sand and sun. Children build sand castles, adults sunbathe, read or listen to radios under umbrellas, and surfers ride the waves along Portugal's

The beach at Albufeira, the Algarve's oldest resort.

magnificent Atlantic coast. While foreign tourists prefer Portugal's most scenic beaches in the Algarve, the Portuguese think more practically and often frequent the beaches closest to home. Although the Algarve coast is visited by 5 million foreign tourists every year, it is also a popular destination of the Portuguese for their summer vacation.

The Outdoors

The Portuguese enjoy nature areas, and they regularly have picnics in parks and go fishing or camping. Strenuous outdoor activities are not quite as popular.

Portugal's nature parks provide many opportunities to get away from the crowds and enjoy a peaceful hike or walk in the woods. Near Lisbon, the Sintra-Cascais Natural Park and the Arrábida Natural Park offer great outdoor activities with romantic castles, ruins, and dense forests. Similarly, the Buçaco National Forest near Coimbra, the Montemuro mountains east of Porto, the Peneda-Gerês National Park near Braga, as well as the Monchique mountains in the Algarve provide similar getaways in a natural and relatively unspoiled setting. Camping is also very popular, and you will find well-kept campgrounds all over Portugal, even in remote areas, where people can spend an affordable vacation in peace and quiet away from the crowds.

SPORTS

Soccer is King

Without a doubt, soccer is Portugal's most popular sport. Although mostly a spectator sport, soccer is also regularly played by many Portuguese on weekends. No matter where you are in Portugal, people gather for informal matches on Sunday afternoons at sports complexes or grassy fields on the outskirts of town. The Portuguese are very passionate about their local teams, and during the national championships, the entire country seems to be divided into rivaling small districts that fiercely favor their team. There are a number of different divisions, from the first division (known as Superliga) with Portugal's best teams to small-town soccer teams that play in regional divisions. Among the best-known teams of the first division are the FC Porto, and the Lisbon teams Benfica and Sporting, all of which continually compete for the title of Portugal's most successful team. Games of these teams incite their fans to much passion, joy, as well as disappointment and fierce debates.

In addition to the games of the various local clubs, the Portuguese fans also follow the matches of the national team with much interest and passion. The Portuguese national team had a few great moments in recent years, especially in the 2000 European Cup, when the Portuguese team reached the semifinals. This success gave rise to the hope for an even better performance during the 2002 Soccer World Cup in Korea and Japan. But much to the dismay of the fans, the Portuguese national team returned home after a disappointing performance in the first round. Perhaps some kind of consolation for Portuguese soccer fans is the fact that Portugal was selected by the Union of European Football Associations (UEFA) to host the 2004 European Championships.

Other Sports Activities

With Portugal's marvelous coastline it is not surprising that water sports are very popular. Many coastal towns, especially in the Algarve have marinas with dozens of moored boats. Surfing is also a popular sport all along the coast. Among the most popular surf spots are the Estremadura coast near Peniche and Nazaré, the coast north and south of Lisbon, and the west coast of the Algarve. Windsurfing is also popular in estuaries and protected areas along the coast, especially in the Eastern Algarve.

Although not a lot of Portuguese are visibly engaged in sports activities, Portuguese athletes continue to attract international attention in several disciplines. In addition to regular successes and titles in European track and field championships, running has become a popular sport. One of Portugal's most popular running events is the annual *Corrida do Tejo*, an 11-km run along the Tejo River in Lisbon.

Bicycle racing is also fairly popular, and Portugal hosts the annual *Volta a Portugal* (Tour of Portugal), which attracts a large number of international participants. For those who like a variety of athletic activities, many towns have sports complexes on the outskirts, usually with swimming pool, track and field facilities, and a soccer field. There are also several upmarket sports such as tennis, golf, and horse riding, which attract more and more locals in addition to foreign visitors. With its growing orientation toward affluent tourists, the Algarve now has a number of golf courses.

Bullfights

Although not nearly as common as in neighboring Spain, bullfighting (known as *festa brava*, or wild feast) is still a popular spectacle in Portugal's cattle-raising regions such as Ribatejo and northern Alentejo. An average of 1.6 million (2001) spectators watch bullfights in Portugal's arenas every year, making the *festa brava* the most popular spectator sport after soccer. The bullfighting festival usually begins with a *largada* (letting loose), when bulls are let loose to run through fenced-off streets, and has its climax in the actual bullfight (*tourada*) in the arena. Portugal developed its own style of *tourada*, where the bull is only fought on horseback by inserting several long rods into the bull's back. It is illegal in Portugal to kill the bull in the arena. A *tourada* can be held in the Portuguese style (on horse), in the Spanish style (on foot), or in the mixed style, where the bull is fought on horse and on foot. But even during bullfights in the Spanish style, the killing of the bull can only be simulated. The bullfighting season starts at Easter and lasts until All Saints' Day. During this period, the various arenas in central Portugal come to life with the excited shouts of the crowd. Vila Franca de Xira, located in northeastern Lisbon, has become famous for its two annual festivals, the Festa do Colete Encarnado (Festival of the Red Waistcoat) in July and the Feira de Outubro (October Fair), complete with bull runs through town and bullfights in the arena.

SOCIALIZING IN PUBLIC

Public Spaces

The mild climate encourages people to be outdoors almost all year round, a fact that is reflected in the social habits of the Portuguese people. Squares, parks, and neighborhood streets are an integral part of the lives of the Portuguese and serve as important gathering places. It is here where people meet neighbors and friends to discuss the day's events or exchange a few friendly words. Women sit out on the alleys and neighborhood streets with their lacework or embroidery, and men meet up for a game of cards or dominoes in a park.

The Rossio Square in Lisbon, a focal meeting point for locals and tourists.

Customers at the Café Majestic in Porto.

Cafés

> *"Grandes cidades paradas nos cafés,*
> *Nos cafés—oasis de inutilidades ruidosas..."*
> (Big cities at a standstill in cafés,
> In cafés— oasis of noisy idleness...)
> —Álvaro de Campos, *Ode Triunfal* (Fernando Pessoa)

Portugal's cafés are lively places where people go for a quick espresso, for a chat with neighbors, and for animated gatherings with friends late at night. Although times have changed since Fernando Pessoa frequented Lisbon's cafés, people still get together until the wee hours of the morning, and his phrase "noisy idleness" still aptly characterizes most of Portugal's cafés today. Although most cafés are simple establishments with a functional décor and neon lighting there are some remarkable exceptions. A few remaining cafés from the early 20th century are among the most elegant and stylish in all of

Europe. These cafés have preserved their art nouveau décor and now stand out as relics of a bygone era of more refined tastes. Every large city has at least one of these vestiges of the golden era of cafés, such as A Brasileira in Lisbon (one of Fernando Pessoa's favorite cafés), the Café Vianna in Braga, the Café Majestic in Porto, and the Café Santa Cruz in Coimbra.

Tea Houses

It was the Portuguese who first brought tea back to Europe from their trading expeditions in the Orient, and it was a Portuguese princess, Catarina de Bragança, who introduced the habit of tea drinking to England, after she married King Charles II of England in 1662. But despite the historic importance of tea in Portugal, it is today much less enjoyed than coffee, which has become the most popular stimulating drink. Tea houses (*casa de chá* or *salão de chá*) were once a popular aristocratic and bourgeois tradition, but only a handful of them remain today. The atmosphere of a tea house is decidedly homier than at the common cafés. The décor is tasteful, the seating comfortable and the lighting pleasantly warm. Among the most popular items at a tea house is the *chá completo* (complete tea), served with a pot of tea and several cookies, pastries, and cakes.

OUT ON THE TOWN

Portugal's cities have a varied and animated nightlife on par with other European cities. The low legal drinking age of 16 ensures that bars and discotheques are crowded with young patrons. People go out late in Portugal, especially on weekends. Most discotheques are open until dawn and only get lively after midnight. Lisbon has doubtlessly the most diverse nightlife in Portugal. The most popular areas to go out to are the Bairro Alto with its many small restaurants, bars, and fado clubs, as well as the so-called Docas area, a revitalized pier under the 25 de Abril Bridge, with restaurants and bars. Porto's nightlife is concentrated near the Cais da Ribeira by the Douro river, and further out by the ocean in Foz do Douro. In contrast, the nightlife in small towns is rather uneventful, since many young people study or work elsewhere. The Algarve coast from Faro to Portimão is one extended party zone during the summer, but almost entirely deserted in the winter.

Bars and Taverns

There are a large variety of drinking establishments in Portugal. The most typical of them all is probably the *tasca*. Most *tascas* are hole-in-the-wall bars, with simple and rustic décor, and often only a handful of tables with wooden benches. In contrast to the lively bars in urban entertainment districts that cater to a diverse crowd, most of the *tascas* are simple neighborhood bars, where the Portuguese, and among them mostly men, gather for conversation over a glass of wine. In addition to these rustic establishments, there is a good number of slightly more upscale bars and taverns. Some cater to the trendy nocturnal crowds with fashionable décor, while others invite with a decidedly ethnic theme or an otherwise unusual and attractive ambience. In wine-growing regions as well as large cities you will also find *adegas*, or wine cellars, which specialize in serving regional wines, usually served from the cask, and a large variety of appetizers.

Dance clubs

Discotheques (*discotecas*) are quite popular among young people and can be found all over Portugal. In small towns, discotheques are often on the outskirts or entirely in the countryside. In cities there are usually concentrations of bars and discotheques in one district or just one street. As elsewhere, discotheques in Portugal cater to the taste and income of their preferred clientele. Some are relatively upscale, with dress code and a high cover charge that usually includes several drinks. Others are more casual and down-to-earth, and cater to a less affluent, but certainly not less lively, student crowd.

Erotic Entertainment and Prostitution

There is little in terms of erotic entertainment in Portugal. There are a few strip clubs, peepshows, and porn shops, as well as *casas de alterne*, where "friendly" women snuggle up to customers and encourage them to have more drinks. In 1962, prostitution was officially outlawed, and all registered brothels were shut down. Prostitution was effectively decriminalized in 1983, but still continues as a clandestine and dangerous activity mainly in seedy parts of towns. There are also illegal *casas de meninas* (brothels) and bars that facilitate meeting women, which are all places that are best avoided.

Living It Up in University Towns

In Portugal's university towns social life is an essential part of academic life. There are numerous traditions and rituals throughout the academic year that liven up Portugal's university towns. The first lively event of the academic year is the traditional *semana da praxe* (week of practice), the first week of the academic year. This is when first-year students, known as *caloiros*, are introduced to their course of study by undergoing a number of comical and humiliating rituals. Accompanied by older students, the *caloiros* walk around town with donkey ears on their heads and carry signs proclaiming their ignorance.

The most important feast of the student year is doubtlessly the Queima das Fitas, the Burning of the Ribbons, a weeklong graduation celebration in May. The most lively Queima das Fitas takes place in Coimbra, when the entire town comes to a standstill. The essential component of this festival is the ritual "burning" of the academic ribbons that identified students as part of their faculty for four years, as a sign that they graduated. This ceremony is preceded by a large procession complete with floats of each faculty, much drinking, dancing, and fun.

THE PERFORMING ARTS

A Diverse Scene

Lisbon, as the capital, has doubtlessly Portugal's most lively performing arts scene, and there are numerous performance venues all over the city. Among the most notable are the Teatro Nacional Dona Maria II (theater productions), the Teatro Nacional São Carlos (concerts and operas), the Centro Cultural de Belém (a varied program of music, dance, exhibits, and theater), and the Coliseu dos Recreios (regular concerts of national and international stars). A notable private institution is the Calouste Gulbenkian Foundation, which has its own concert hall with an orchestra, choir, and ballet and hosts numerous performances of dance, music, and theater. Porto is home to Portugal's second largest performing arts scene. The main performance venues are the Rivoli Teatro Municipal, the Coliseu do Porto, and the Teatro Nacional São João. Many small towns also host concerts, music festivals, and theater performances.

Portugal has several ballet and dance ensembles which have a steady presence in performing arts venues in Lisbon, Porto, and elsewhere. Among them are the Companhia Portuguesa de Bailado Contemporâneo, the Companhia de Dança de Lisboa, the Companhia Nacional de Bailado (CNB), and the Ballet Gulbenkian, which all perform both classical ballets as well as experimental and modern choreographies. The Companhia Paulo Ribeiro is among Portugal's best-known small dance companies, and it always surprises with new and experimental projects.

Portugal only has a small tradition in theater and drama. Nonetheless, every Portuguese city has at least one stately theater and several small stages with a diverse and interesting repertoire. The plays of 16th century dramatist Gil Vicente are still widely popular and his plays are still regularly performed all over the country. Portugal's theater productions include many international plays, and plays by contemporary Portuguese playwrights are also regularly performed especially at the many small stages, which often have a more experimental scope than the large national theaters.

Movie Theaters

There are movie theaters in every Portuguese city, usually in commercial districts and shopping centers. In smaller towns, multi-purpose performance halls are used for weekly or biweekly movie showings. Porto and Lisbon have the most diverse selection of film venues. Among the venues that have alternative festivals and show films outside the mainstream are the Cinemateca Portuguesa, the Videoteca Municipal, the Cine Paraíso, and the Cinema 222, all in Lisbon. Universities, as well as cultural centers and institutions, also have film showings from time to time. In Porto, the Casa das Artes as well as the Museu Serralves have a diverse offering of films, both classic and recent. At many movie theaters across Portugal, movie tickets are discounted on Mondays.

Finding Out What's Going On

To find out about the cultural events in Portugal's cities and towns, check the newspapers, most of which have a pullout on weekends that lists cultural events. Porto and Lisbon also publish their own free monthly calendar of events, called Agenda do Porto and Agenda Cultural Lisboa respectively. These entertainment guides are available at tourist offices and museums.

Chapter Eleven

MOVING TO PORTUGAL

*"Isto é uma terra de gente que partiu para o mar. É o lugar
ideal para perder alguém ou para perder-se de si próprio."*
(This is a land of people who departed for the sea. It is the
ideal place to lose someone or to lose oneself.)
—From the movie *Terra Estrangeira* (Foreign Land)
by Walter Salles

BEFORE YOU LEAVE HOME

What should you bring?
If you plan to spend an extended period of time in Portugal, it is

probably worth making a list of essential items to bring along. As a EU country most common consumer goods are available in Portugal, and it won't be necessary to bring household goods that can be easily purchased in Portugal. Portugal produces clothing and shoes of good value, and you don't have to stock up on these items before leaving your home country. On the other hand, English books are hard to find, especially outside urban areas, and the selection is small. If you enjoy reading, and your Portuguese is not yet good enough to read José Saramago's novels in their original language, you should probably bring at least a few good novels. If you come from North America, keep in mind that the electric current in Portugal is 220 volts, 50 cycles. If you would like to bring electronics or other electrical equipment, purchase a transformer that has enough amperage to handle your equipment. When bringing television equipment or videotapes, be aware that Portuguese television uses the PAL system, which is not compatible with the North American NTSC system.

Practicalities of the Move

If you will be living in Portugal for a while, you might want to consider a mail forwarding service that redirects your mail to your new overseas location. Choosing a power of attorney and making your bank and credit card accounts at home accessible via Internet may also ease your move abroad. Automatic payment service is also a great tool to make sure that your bills at home are paid while you are away.

There are several other issues you should research before getting ready to move abroad. Among them are schooling for your children, shipment of your automobile, exploring the housing/rental market at your destination, or contacting a relocation company or agent. You should also have the visas and work permits for your family arranged well ahead of time to avoid complications and delays. Friends of mine had requested their US passports by mail about two months before their Portugal trip, but they waited until the last week to inquire why they had not yet received them. Apparently the birth certificate on one application was missing, and my friends had to pay for rush service to get their passports on time for their Lisbon flight. Without any doubt the most expensive part of moving abroad will be shipping your belongings, especially household goods. Depending on how much you value these items, it might be better to store your furniture at home and buy or rent furniture in Portugal. Another option is renting a furnished apartment.

ENTRY REQUIREMENTS

General Requirements

Citizens of the EU only need an identification card to enter Portugal and citizens of most other European countries can enter Portugal with a valid passport. This also applies to citizens of the USA, Canada, Australia and several other countries, who can enter Portugal with a passport that is valid for at least three months beyond their intended stay in Portugal. Citizens of all other countries should contact a Portuguese consulate and inquire about specific entry requirements that may apply.

As part of the Schengen Convention that took effect in 1995 and eliminated border controls, the EU (except the UK and Ireland), as well as Norway and Iceland, has agreed to a common immigration policy. In general, if you are not a EU citizen, you are allowed to spend up to 90 days out of every six months in the countries covered by the Schengen treaty. This means that legally, after spending 90 days in Portugal, you have to leave the Schengen area for 90 days, after which you could return to Portugal for another 90 days. An extension of your legal 90-day stay in Portugal is possible by applying at an office of the *Serviço de Estrangeiros e Fronteiras* (SEF), the Service of Foreigners and Borders. Be prepared to present a valid reason for wanting to extend your stay. If you overstay the legal limit of your stay, you will be fined according to the number of days you overstayed. For information on how to contact the SEF in Portugal, see the Resource Guide chapter in this book. Citizens of non-EU countries who are interested in staying in Portugal for the purpose of study or employment need to contact a Portuguese consulate in their home country before their arrival in Portugal and make arrangements for a work or student visa.

Customs Regulations

There are no restrictions for EU citizens on what and how much they bring to Portugal from another EU country, as long as the items are for personal use or consumption. Citizens of non-EU countries can bring with them 200 cigarettes, 1 liter of spirits or two liters of wine, or beer. It is prohibited to bring fresh meat to Portugal. Foreign visitors from outside the EU are allowed to bring personal items that are exempt from import duties. This includes electronic equipment such as cameras, CD players, or laptop computers. There is no limit on how much foreign currency can be brought into Portugal. Foreigners who plan to temporarily or permanently move to Portugal should inquire at a Portuguese consulate about regulations regarding the importation of household goods, personal belongings, and professional equipment.

Vaccination Requirements

No vaccinations are required for travelers entering continental Portugal. However, travelers need to carry a yellow fever vaccination certificate, if they arrive in the Azores or Madeira from infected areas, such as some countries in Africa and South America. Passengers merely in transit on these islands do not need a certificate.

Bringing Pets

If you intend to bring your pet to Portugal it is best to contact the Portuguese consulate or embassy for detailed information. In general, you will need an updated health and vaccination certificate (including a rabies certificate) from a recognized veterinarian dated shortly before the day of travel, which has to be certified by the Portuguese consulate in your country.

DOCUMENTATION AND OTHER FORMALITIES

Residency Permits

There are no restrictions for EU citizens with regard to living in Portugal, and in theory they can stay as long as they want. But those who want to establish official residency in Portugal need to apply for a residency permit *(residência)* and meet several requirements. In order to obtain Portuguese residency (regardless if you are a EU citizen or not), you must be either employed or self-employed in Portugal, or have retirement income (or another form of income) from abroad. If you are retired and would like to live in Portugal, you need to prove that your pension is large enough to support you in Portugal. You also need to show proof of medical insurance, so that you will not become a burden to the state. If you are employed or self-employed in Portugal you automatically make contributions to social security and are eligible for free medical services in Portugal. To initiate the process of obtaining residency as a EU citizen you need to contact an office of the SEF in Portugal. Foreigners from outside the EU need to contact a Portuguese consulate in their home country to find about the different options for visas. Most residency visas issued to foreigners are temporary permits that need to be renewed every year. Usually after five years a temporary residency permit can be converted to permanent residency. For information on work visas, see the respective section in the Work and Business chapter in this book.

Tax Identification Card

If you will be working and paying taxes in Portugal, or if you want to open a bank account, you need to get a tax identification card *(cartão de identificação fiscal*). You can apply for a tax number at the local tax office, often located at the local town hall (*junta de freguesia*). You will be assigned a *número fiscal de contribuinte*, i.e. a tax number. You will receive a temporary document when you first apply for your tax number. The final document will be sent to you by mail within a few months.

Driver's License

If you are a EU citizen and live in Portugal, you can use the driver's license of your home country without any restrictions or time limits. Other foreign citizens are allowed to drive with their national driver's license for up to six months, after which they are required to get a Portuguese driver's license. An international driver's license can be useful, since it contains a Portuguese or Spanish translation of your national driver's license. All foreign residents of Portugal are required to get a Portuguese *cartão de condução* (driver's license) as soon as they register a car in Portugal. This applies to both EU citizens and those from other countries. You can apply for a driver's license at any office of the *Direcção-Geral de Viação*, the General Traffic Administration, located in every district capital and many towns. Taking a driver's test is generally not necessary.

Bringing a Car

You can legally drive your car in Portugal with a foreign registration for 180 days. After that you need to apply for Portuguese license plates. If you plan to move to Portugal and establish residency you may be able to import your car as part of your household belongings. However, if you are already a resident of Portugal and would like to import a vehicle you have elsewhere, you have to go through a lengthy importation process and pay certain taxes.

Registering with your Consulate

It is a good idea for any foreign national to register with their consulate after arriving in Portugal. This will make it easier to help you in case your passport is stolen, or in case you need other assistance from your consulate. If your passport is lost or stolen, report the incident to your consulate as soon as possible. Your consulate may also be able to assist you with finding medical help and with forwarding money from your family back home.

SETTING UP HOME

Settling in a new country is a lengthy and often stressful process. It is not only about leaving your old home behind and tying up loose ends, but also about successfully settling at your new location. This section provides some guidelines to make this important step of setting up home in Portugal a little easier.

Looking for Housing

Unless you have contacts or an employer who will assist you with your apartment search, the newspaper *classificados* (classifieds) will be your best choice in your search for housing. Check under *habitações* (apartments), *moradias* (homes), *quartos* (rooms), or *casas* (houses), or look for the *Alugam-se* (for rent) or *arrendamento* (rental) heading. You will find a large selection of available rentals with numerous options: furnished or unfurnished, with or without garage, with or wihout a fully equipped kitchen, central heating or no heating at all. Real estate agencies (*mediadoras imobiliárias*) may also be able to assist you in finding an apartment or home. When describing the size of an apartment, the term *assoalhada* is frequently used and means 'room'. Apartment sizes are often abbreviated with the letter T followed by a number that indicates the number of bedrooms. T0 (T zero) is a studio apartment, or *estúdio* (with no separate bedroom), T1 is a one-bedroom apartment with living room and kitchen, T2 is a two-bedroom apartment with living room and kitchen, and so on.

General Considerations

The main consideration for renting a house in any city should be its location. In Lisbon and Porto especially, commuter time is an important factor when looking for an apartment. If you are a student or know where you will work, you can pick a location that is close to your university or job. Also keep in mind the distance to commercial areas, shopping centers, and to parks or playgrounds if you have children. Find out about public transportation, especially if you don't have a vehicle. And if you have a car, find out if a garage is available. Parking is a nightmare in Portugal's cities, and living close to public transportation is essential. Since streets are often congested and buses and trams move slowly, living close to a subway or commuter train in Lisbon and Porto will save you a lot of time. Also keep in mind the noise factor, when selecting a home, and be aware of busy streets with traffic going by day and night. A friend of mine lived in an apartment

163

close to Lisbon's cathedral and several other churches, and sleeping in on Sunday morning was impossible because of the chimes. Apartments in older buildings often have windows that open out onto tiny courtyards, and noises from neighbors above, below, and across are easily heard. This is also true for the smell of food, like fried sardines on a late Sunday morning for example, when one might be getting ready to enjoy a delicious cup of coffee. Fortunately, the Portuguese are for the most part considerate and quiet people, and you will rarely have to deal with more than just incidental noise.

There are a few peculiarities about the Portuguese housing and rental market that foreigners should be aware of. For one thing, single-family homes and houses to rent are rare and difficult to find. Most living situations that are ready to be rented are apartments or condominiums in apartment buildings or complexes. An increasingly popular phenomenon are gated apartment complexes and high-rises, complete with security guards and parking garages. This type of living situation is comparatively expensive and is usually located on the outskirts of cities in more affluent suburbs. Their low-income counterparts are the rather somber housing projects scattered on the outskirts of Portugal's cities, which are best avoided. Portugal's cities have hundreds of centrally located older apartment buildings, but unfortunately few old apartments are rented in a renovated state. Apartments in older buildings are charming, with tall ceilings, large windows and wrought-iron balconies, but they often involve a lot of work to move in.

Central heating is very rare, and only available in some new or renovated apartments. Apparently most people don't consider the winters long or cold enough to justify such an investment, and they use electric space or portable gas heaters in their apartments. Other details to look out for when looking at places to rent are cupboards, storage and pantry space, a balcony (for hanging clothes) as well as hook up for a washing machine.

The rental price of a house or apartment also reflects the overall reputation of the neighborhood it is located in, and you should look for an apartment in a safe neighborhood that you like. Expect substantial differences between an unrenovated apartment in an older building, and a renovated or even fairly new apartment. Rentals in urban areas are also higher than in small towns, which is why a lot of people from lower income groups live in the suburbs around Lisbon and Porto.

The Rental Contract

Rental contracts are usually signed for at least a year, and often for longer. If you plan to spend less time, you should probably look for a sublet. It is customary for tenants to pay a *caução* (security deposit), which is at least the value of one month's rent, possibly more. Some landlords require a *fiador* (guarantor), who will be responsible for rent payment, in case the tenant fails to pay. Before signing a contract, make sure you understand your rights and obligations in case of an early termination of the contract and other disputes that may arise. Most towns have a renters' association *(associação de inquilinos)* which helps renters with legal aspects of contracts and rentals. Rent control laws are in effect all over Portugal, and every year the government determines the percentage of small rent increases, which usually corresponds to the inflation rate.

Utilities in Your Home

Water

Aguas de Portugal, still controlled by the government, provides running water to most households in Portugal. Tap water is treated and is generally considered safe for drinking. However, if you do not like the taste of treated water, bottled drinking water is readily available at grocery stores. Some towns in the interior suffer water shortages during summer droughts, and the water quality deteriorates during this period.

Gas

The majority of Portuguese households use gas for cooking and water heating, and most homes and apartments in cities have access to gas lines. In smaller towns or rural areas however, gas lines are not as common, and water heaters and kitchen stoves are operated by large gas bottles that are sold at gas stations, stores, or private homes.

Electricity

Electric power is provided by EDP, Electricidade de Portugal, S.A., once a government enterprise, but now largely privatized. Power surges and blackouts do occur from time to time, especially in small towns and remote areas, but the power supply is generally very reliable. The electric current in Portugal is 220 volts, 50 hertz. Portugal uses the same type of plug as all of continental Europe.

DOMESTIC HELP

Although only affluent families have full-time maids in Portugal, household help ((known as *mulher-a-dias*) hired for a day or two per week is quite common. Depending on your situation and income level, this may be a suitable option for you. Salary levels are very low in Portugal compared to most other EU countries, and a maid *(criada* or *mulher-a-dias)* is probably much more affordable in Portugal than in your home country. If you decide to hire household help, it is best to ask friends or coworkers for a recommendation, since it is not always easy to find reliable domestic help. Word of mouth usually works better than going the more official way of going through classified ads or employment agencies.

INITIAL ADJUSTMENTS

Culture Shock in Portugal?

When I told friends that I was working on a book called *Culture*

Shock! Portugal, many of them asked me: "Is it possible to experience culture shock in Portugal?" Well, in fact, it is. Portugal is perhaps not drastically different from other western European countries, but culture shock not only manifests itself in countries where the locals paint their faces, wear strange costumes, and practice exotic religious rites. Culture shock is an experience that becomes evident in the little daily routines, and is made up of the many small differences of daily life in another country. Culture shock is the lack of familiarity, the lack of known places, faces and customs. Culture shock gradually creeps up on the newcomer, and usually happens after the initial excitement has worn off. Overwhelmed by an unfamiliar culture and a language they don't understand, foreigners often react with homesickness, stress and anxiety. While some degree of culture shock is natural and inevitable, foreigners can avoid a lot of adjustment difficulties by planning well ahead.

Prepare Yourself

Among the first steps to take, regardless of the purpose of your stay in Portugal, is to learn the language. I met several foreign students in Lisbon who took an intensive language course in Portugal before studying as an exchange student at a university. They had a great advantage over those students who only arrived in Portugal at the beginning of the academic year. Similarly, for someone with a professional mission in Portugal, it would be a good idea to study at least the basics of the language before having to speak it. It is also very helpful to get in-depth information about the country you will be living in. The more you can find out about the Portuguese and their culture before your arrival, the easier the adjustment period will be for you. Perhaps someone you know has lived in Portugal, or you may know one of the many Portuguese emigrants living abroad. Take advantage of such contacts to ask questions and get a better idea of what to expect. The Resource Guide lists recommended books and websites to further deepen your knowledge about Portugal.

167

Sharing Your Experiences

No matter if they are retirees, students, or professionals, most foreigners initially prefer the company of people from their own cultural background and only gradually make contact with the Portuguese. This is quite natural, since most newcomers speak little Portuguese and are simply not able to communicate well with the locals. Sharing their first impressions and experiences with other foreigners helps them bridge this initial period of adjustment and deal better with the frustrating aspects of living in Portugal. A good example is probably the inflated bureaucracy and the slight but ever-so-present inefficiency that prevails in so many aspects of public life. A friend of mine was waiting in line at a Lisbon public transport office to apply for his monthly bus pass. When he got to the counter after a long wait, he was told that they could not accept his application because it was written in blue ink instead of black. Since none of the employees could lend him a black pen, he had to leave and return another day. What could be a better way to get over this experience than to share it with your friends and laugh about it? While such incidences are doubtlessly frustrating, it is important to take your initial experiences lightly. Most of them are little more than minor annoyances, and they are not worth losing your sleep over. An open mind, a fair amount of patience, and a good sense of humor are probably your best survival tools in Portugal. With a positive attitude you will be able to quickly disregard little daily annoyances and focus more on the pleasant aspects of living in Portugal.

Meeting the Locals

Living in a foreign country and having little or no contact with the locals is a missed opportunity. It is easy to remain within the safe confines of an expatriate community, but if the companionship of other expatriates is so essential, why leave one's home country in the first place? It is not only the climate and the scenery that make a country attractive. It may sound redundant, but more than anything else it is the people that make the country what it is. If you like Portuguese food, music, or art, it is certainly worth meeting the people who over the centuries have created the delicious meals and wine, who have invented the cheerful folkloric dances, and built these marvelous churches and castles. No doubt, meeting the local people is difficult at first because of the different language, but making local friends is always a rewarding experience. By getting to know the locals you will gain a better understanding of the Portuguese people and their culture, which will immensely enrich your time in Portugal.

Portugal for Children

Portugal must be one of the better countries in Europe for children. Children are welcome everywhere and most Portuguese are very tolerant and patient with children. Portuguese children also seem to have a tad more freedom to play where and how they please.

Regardless of your own approach to pedagogical issues, rest assured that your children will be welcome in Portugal, and that they will be easily accepted by both Portuguese adults and the local children they meet. Still, the adjustment to a new environment will also be a challenge for your children, and it is important to talk to them about the changes that await them in Portugal. Maintaining some familiarities during this transition is probably the best you can do. This will help them get used to the new life without completely leaving their favorite games, toys, or activities. Depending on how long you are planning to stay in Portugal, it may be a good idea to expose them to Portuguese culture and language sooner rather than later. The sooner your children have contact with local children, the sooner they will be able to cope with the language shock, make friends, and start fitting in.

EXPATRIATES IN PORTUGAL

Most of the 240,000 legal foreigners in Portugal are immigrants from Africa and Brazil, who come to Portugal to work and save money, as well as EU citizens who come to Portugal for a variety of reasons. In 2002 there were 61,000 EU citizens in Portugal, mostly from Great Britain, Spain, France, and Germany. In addition to the 15,000 British residents, there are also about 10,000 residents from Canada and 8,000 from the USA, to give you an idea of Portugal's contingent of English speakers. Lisbon certainly has the highest expatriate population in Portugal with communities of citizens from all Western European countries, all well as from North America and Portuguese-speaking countries such as Cabo Verde, Angola, and Brazil. Lisbon and Coimbra also have a considerable foreign student population, usually on a one-year student exchange at a Portuguese university. There are about 31,000 foreign residents in the Algarve, over half of them from the EU. With its mild climate, southern Portugal is especially popular with senior citizens from Northern European countries during the winter months. Numerous foreigners, especially from Great Britain and Germany, have settled in the Algarve to retire or to open businesses related to tourism. Outside the Algarve, Lisbon, and Porto there are only scattered foreign residents in Portugal.

Making Contacts

Getting connected to an expatriate community is a good way of making first contacts in Portugal. Expatriates are usually helpful to newcomers from their own culture or country, and you might get important leads regarding housing or work and receive useful advice and assistance. In the cities and towns of the Algarve, the expatriate communities are fairly small and people get to know each other quickly. In larger cities such as Lisbon or Porto, you may need to pursue more formal channels to make contacts with expatriates, possibly through your consulate, Chamber of Commerce, or English-speaking social clubs. There are several websites and publications for English-speaking residents in Portugal, which advertise services, rental, work opportunities, and contact information for the expatriate community. The Resource Guide lists both online and printed resources for expatriates in Portugal.

Chapter Twelve

DAILY LIFE

"A cada dia dá Deus a dor e a alegria."
(Every day God gives pain and joy.)

—Portuguese saying

SHOPPING

Buying Groceries

For daily grocery needs, Portugal is well stocked with small grocery stores called *mercearias*. They provide all the essentials, from bread and cheese to fruit, laundry soap, and wine and are found in most neighborhoods. One step up in size are the *supermercados* (supermarkets), where the selection is a little better and the prices are lower. Among the most common supermarket chains you will come across are Minipreço, Ponto Fresco, Pingo Doce, and Lidl. Large discount supermarkets, which sell more than just groceries, are known as *hipermercados*. The most popular ones are Carrefour, Intermarché (Os Mosqueteiros), and Continente, often located on the outskirts of towns near shopping centers.

Markets and Fairs

Markets and fairs are very popular events all over Portugal, and people flock to them in large crowds. Cities may have a market hall for the daily or weekly market, and smaller towns reserve a large square in the center for that purpose. These markets are a great showcase of regional produce and food specialities. Much of the fruit and vegetables are grown locally, and the cheese and meat products

A produce seller at the local market.

are often home-made. The market in Barcelos, *feira de Barcelos*, held every Wednesday, is one of Portugal's largest and most popular markets and is especially famous for the typical red ceramic, which is produced locally. In addition to regular markets, each town has a number of fairs, often held in conjunction with religious festivals or other events such as agricultural shows or bullfights. These fairs are very lively events and often feature livestock, agricultural products, and local handicrafts and are always accompanied by music, dance, and folkloric performances.

Retail Stores and Shopping Centers

Portugal is a country where the downtown shopping districts still consist mostly of small retail stores. Such stores are often owner-operated, and each customer is personally assisted by an employee. Large retail chains and department stores are mostly found in shopping centers on the outskirts of town. Most cities have at least one *centro commercial (*shopping center), replete with restaurants, dozens of stores, and movie theaters. Lisbon's Centro Comercial Colombo is the largest shopping center on the Iberian Peninsula with 420 shops and over 60 restaurants. Most stores are open from 9:00am to 1:00pm and 3:00pm to 6:00pm or 7:00pm on weekdays, and from 9:00am to 1:00pm on Saturdays. Most retail stores are closed on Sundays. Shopping centers in cities are generally open seven days a week.

POSTAL SERVICE

The national postal service is Correios de Portugal, which you will recognize by the bright red Correios sign. There is usually a post office in the center of town and in every city district. Opening hours are usually Monday to Friday, from 9:00am to noon and from 2:00pm to 6:00pm. In urban areas, the post offices do not close for lunch and may be open on Saturdays from 9:00am to 1:00pm. There are two types of basic mail service in Portugal: *correio normal* (normal service) and *correio azul* (priority service), both available for domestic and international mailings. In addition to these standard services, *encomenda prioritária internacional* (international express mail service) is also available, as well as insured and registered mail. Mailboxes around town are bright red, and in many places the old, red, cylindrical cast-iron mailboxes are still in use. For priority mail drop (with higher postage), use the blue *correio azul* mailboxes. Post offices also offer fax and telex service, as well as Internet access. In addition to the Portuguese postal service there are also several other courier companies such as DHL and Fedex.

TELECOMMUNICATIONS

Since the privatization of Portugal's telephone system in 2000, telephone services have been improved and modernized. Portugal Telecom (PT) Comunicações is Portugal's largest telecommunications company and controls the market.

Residential Telephones

To have a residential telephone line (*telefone fixo*) installed in your home, contact a PT office. There is usually a one-time installation fee as well as monthly service charges. In Portugal phone calls are charged by the pulse, and the number of pulses per minute depends on the time of day and the location you are calling. Most telephone wall jacks in Portugal use the RJ-11 plug type common in North America, but there is also an older plug type that is still in use. The RJ-11 plug works with laptops or any other computer.

Public Telephones

Public phone booths are operated either by coins or by telephone card, known as *telecom card*. These electronic cards come in a number of different denominations and are available at PT telephone offices, post offices, newsstands, and tobacconists. Most post offices provide

175

phone booths for long distance and international calls. PT also has telephone offices for long-distance calls, Internet access, as well as other services.

Telephone Cards

Prepaid telephone cards are also available, mostly for international phone calls. They work with a toll-free number and an access code, and can be used from any telephone. Companies such as Marconi and PT offer calling cards in several different denominations, available at newsstands, post offices, and PT offices.

Cellular Telephones

Cellular telephones (called *telemóvel*) are immensely popular in Portugal and have almost achieved the status of a cult object. Whether you are on a bus, in a restaurant, or walking down the street, there will always be someone busily talking on a cell phone next to you. In addition to cell phones with regular monthly service charges, cell phones with prepaid cards are also very popular, since it is easier to budget expenditures. If you don't have a residential telephone line or won't stay in Portugal for very long, your best bet is to purchase a cell phone that works with a prepaid telephone card. If you bring a cell phone from another European country to Portugal, you should inquire about local cellular service. Depending on the manufacturer, you may be able to simply purchase a Portuguese telephone chip and start using a local service provider. Due to different cellular systems and frequencies, cell phones from North America do not work in Portugal. At the time of writing (2003), there were three cell phone companies operating in Portugal: TMN, Vodafone Telecel, and Optimus.

Making Phone Calls Within Portugal

Area codes are no longer in use. Domestic numbers are now nine digits long, which must all be dialed regardless of where you are calling in Portugal. Reduced telephone charges apply from 9pm to 9am and on Saturdays, Sundays, and holidays.

Collect Calls

To make a collect call within Portugal, dial 120, and wait for an operator to assist you. Be aware that collect calls are quite expensive compared to regular phone calls. International collect calls from Portugal can be made by dialing the toll-free access number for the country you want you call. This will connect you to an English-speaking operator who will set up the collect call for you.

Australia: 800 800 610
Canada: 800 800 122
United Kingdom: 800 800 440
USA:
via ATT : 800 800 128
via MCI: 800 800 123
via Sprint: 800 800 187

International Calls

When calling Portugal from abroad, first dial the international access number, then the country code 351. Since area codes are no longer in use, simply dial the entire nine-digit telephone number after the country code. To make an international phone call from Portugal, first dial the international access code 00, then the country code, area code, and phone number. For information about international phone calls, dial 179; for operator-assisted international phone calls, dial 171. Just like phone calls within Portugal, international calls have reduced rates on weekends.

Selected country codes, as dialed from Portugal:
Australia: 00-61
Canada: 00-1

United Kingdom: 00-44
USA: 00-1

Directory Assistance

Automated assistance: 118
Operator assistance: 12118, or via Internet: net118.telecom.pt
International directory assistance: 177

Faxes

Faxes can be sent from post offices, PT telephone offices, and most hotels. Since international faxes are charged at the regular rates of international phone calls they are quite expensive, especially when sent during business hours.

FINANCIAL MATTERS

> *"O dinheiro é sempre o mesmo, os bolsos é que mudam."*
> (The money is always the same, it is the pockets that change.)
>
> —Portuguese saying

On January 1, 2002, the euro replaced Portugal's long-time currency, the escudo. Although the escudo is no longer in circulation, many people continue to use it as a reference to what things cost, especially when talking about expensive items such as cars or houses. Eventually there will be less mention of the escudo, as the euro becomes a more familiar currency and reference point for the Portuguese.

Foreign Exchange

The best places to exchange foreign currency is a *casa de câmbio* (exchange house). They are commonly found in tourist areas such as the Algarve and in large cities, but are hard to find elsewhere.

Exchange houses accept both cash and traveler's checks, and many of them are open seven days a week until late at night. Many banks also exchange foreign currencies, but they usually charge high fees. To avoid surprises, compare the rates and commissions of banks and exchange houses before changing large amounts of money. Traveler's checks are a safe way to carry money, but a commission is charged when purchasing them, and the exchange rate is lower than that of cash. Most banks are open Monday to Friday from 8:30am to 3:00pm. They are closed on weekends and official holidays. In small towns, banks may close during lunch hour, usually from noon to 2:00pm.

Automatic Teller Machines

Foreign currency withdrawals from bank machines (*caixa automático*) are the most economic form of currency exchange. Bank machines are open 24 hours a day, the exchange rate is better than for cash, and the fees are lower than at an exchange house or bank. The most common automated cashier system in Portugal is called Multibanco (MB), a nationwide network that serves most banks. These cash machines can be found outside banks, in bank lobbies, at railway and subway stations, and at shopping centers. They usually accept cards with a variety of symbols, such as Mastercard/Eurocard/Cirrus, Maestro, Visa/Plus, Visa Electron, American Express, and EC (Eurocheque).

Credit Cards

Credit cards are not as widely accepted as in other EU countries, but an increasing number of shops now display the Visa, Mastercard, American Express, and Diner's Club symbols, especially in areas with international tourism, commercial districts, and shopping centers. Always be prepared to pay cash at small guesthouses, restaurants, and shops, especially in small towns and rural areas. Debit cards or check cards with the Visa or Mastercard logo can be used in the same way as credit cards.

Money Transfers

Most banks will receive money wires, if you need money sent to you in Portugal. They are usually processed within a few working days. All you need is the routing number of the Portuguese bank where you would like to receive the funds. The best thing is to select a centrally located bank and get the details at the customer service counter. Money wired to Portugal is paid out in euros. The postal service (Correios) and exchange houses (such as Cotacâmbios) use the Western Union network for fast international money transfers. Some foreign consulates (including the USA) process money transfers for their citizens for a fee. Inquire at your consulate if you are in need of such an emergency transfer.

Bank Accounts

To open a bank account in Portugal, you need identification (a passport, or for EU citizens an identification card), in addition to a tax number, the *número do contribuinte*. You can apply for a tax number at the local tax office. There are a variety of bank accounts with varying services and fees, from simple savings accounts to checking accounts with Multibanco cards and overdraft protection. Since the European Central Bank (ECB) determines the interest rates for all countries of the euro zone, interest rates of Portuguese credit cards vary little from those in other EU countries.

Paying Your Bills

Since customer service at banks is slow and lines are long, making payments for your monthly bills at an ATM is a very attractive option. Most of the common monthly utilities can be paid at bank machines by using your Portuguese Multibanco card and entering the necessary information provided on the bill.

THE MEDIA

Newspapers and Magazines

Portugal has a large number of newspapers. All district capitals and many small towns have their own daily or weekly publication. Portugal's largest and most reputable daily newspapers are *Diário de Notícias*, *Jornal de Notícias* from Porto, and *O Público*. There are also a number of weekly newspapers, such as *Expresso* and *O Independente*, as well as the weekly news magazines *Focus* and *Visão*, with a broad coverage of domestic and international news. Among the most common English-language publications sold at newsstands are *The Guardian*, *The Times*, *The Independent*, *The International Herald Tribune*, *USA Today*, *The Economist*, and *Time* magazine. There are a few weekly English-language newspapers published in Portugal, including *APN* (Anglo-Portuguese News) and *The Portugal News*.

Bookstores

Good bookstores are hard to find in small towns, but Porto, Coimbra, and Lisbon have veritable book districts, with a dozen or more bookstores within a few blocks. In Porto, the area just below the old university, the old center of Coimbra, and the Chiado district in Lisbon are home to Portugal's most diverse and interesting bookstores. Second-hand bookstores, known as *alfarrabistas*, are also quite an enjoyable experience for bookworms. A good selection of English books is not easy to find in Portugal. Although most bookstores carry some English titles, the selection is often limited to works commonly needed by students. Try the larger bookstores such as Bertrand Livreiros (with 30 branches in Portugal), the French electronics/media chain FNAC, or the eclectic Livraria Buchholz in Lisbon.

Television and Radio

There are four free-to-air TV channels in Portugal: the government channels Rádio Televisão Portuguesa (RTP) 1 and 2, and the private channels SIC and TVI. Portugal's local TV production is small and does not exceed a small number of *telenovelas* (soap operas), TV series, and news programs. The majority of movies on Portuguese TV are foreign and are shown in their original version with Portuguese subtitles. The most popular TV programs are Brazilian soap operas, talk and game shows, as well as sitcoms. Cable and satellite TV now offer several movie channels with English-language movies, as well as BBC World Service TV.

Portugal's main radio stations are Antenna 1, Antenna 2, and Antenna 3, which belong to the government broadcasting system RDP (Rádio Difusão Portuguesa). There are also several private radio stations, some of which are only aired locally. Among them are Radio Renascença, Radio Cidade, TSF, and Radio Nostalgia.

Internet

Although not as widely used as in most other Western European countries, the Internet has experienced rapid growth in the past few years. Among the largest providers of dial-up and broadband access are Sapo (www.sapo.pt), Telepac (www.telepac.pt), Clix Turbo (www.clix.pt), and Oninet (www.oninet.pt). There are also companies that provide Internet access through television cables. Public Internet access is available for free in many towns at public libraries and through the Espaço Internet program. Internet cafés, Portugal Telecom centers, and the Netpost stations at post offices charge a modest fee to connect to the Internet.

GETTING AROUND

Taxi

Taxis can be hailed on the street, found at taxi stands, or called by telephone. Taxis in Portugal are now beige in color, although a few old green and black ones are still around. In small towns you will mostly find A taxis, which do not have a sign on the roof but display the letter A on the door. These taxis, mainly for rural traffic, do not use a meter, but charge a fare according to distance. A tip of 10% of the fare is customary.

Buses and Streetcars

Portugal's cities all have a well-developed public transport system, mostly buses. In Porto and Lisbon, a few streetcar lines remain from the old days but they are plagued with delays caused by cars parked too close to the tracks. Still, even though buses are faster, a visit to Lisbon would not be complete without a ride in one of the old streetcars. It also happens that these streetcars lead through some of

A streetcar climbing a hill in Lisbon.

Lisbon's most charming neighborhoods, such as Alfama, Mouraria, Graça, and the Bairro Alto. Tickets purchased in advance are much cheaper than those bought on the bus or streetcar.

Subway

The Lisbon subway (*metro*) has four lines that connect outer districts with the city center. It is in operation from about 6am to 1am, with less frequent service on weekends and holidays. For the metro you can buy single or multiple-ride tickets, as well as a three-day tourist pass and a monthly pass. A suburban train service called Metro Sul do Tejo (MST) that heads to destinations south of the Tejo River is in the planning stages. Three light rail lines are planned for Porto, which are scheduled to be completed by 2006. They will connect suburbs and surrounding cities with Porto, with several underground stops in Porto's city center.

Long-Distance Bus Travel

Express routes between Portugal's major cities use modern buses, and service is fairly efficient and fast. On the other hand, getting around rural Portugal takes much flexibility, patience, time, and sometimes, tenacity. Each region has its major bus companies that connect the major towns, but connections to another region or district are often slow with numerous layovers. While it is certainly worthwhile and rewarding to explore Portugal's remote villages and towns, getting to your destination by bus can be frustrating and time-consuming.

Railroads

With the exception of regional routes, trains are a comfortable and speedy way of travel in Portugal. Rail service connects all major cities, and some regional routes in the interior are also still in operation. The Portuguese Railways (Caminhos de Ferro Portugueses) offer a variety of special fare tickets, and it is a good idea to ask about special promotions before purchasing a ticket. A high-speed railway between Madrid and Lisbon is in the planning stages. There will also be a high-speed railroad from Porto north to the Spanish city of Vigo.

Air Travel

TAP (Transportes Aéreos Portugueses) is Portugal's national airline, which is still partly owned by the government. Continental Portugal has three international airports, the Francisco Sá Carneiro airport in Porto, the Lisbon International (or Portela) Airport, and the Faro International Airport. Portugal's airports are fairly small by international standards and are easy to get around in. Although neither Lisbon nor Porto are major European hubs for international airlines, several European and North American airlines have regular flight service to and from Portugal. Portugal's airports are connected to city centers by regular shuttle and bus service.

DRIVING IN PORTUGAL

Driving in Portugal is not for the meek or feeble. Portuguese driving habits are somewhat erratic, and it is best to prepare for anarchic traffic conditions. Speed limits, stop signs, and no-passing zones are generally disregarded. Portugal has one of the worst driving statistics in the EU and one of the highest accident rates on highways.

Rules and Regulations

To legally drive your foreign car in Portugal you need a valid identification card (or passport), your driver's license, the vehicle registration, a sticker identifying the nationality of your vehicle and proof of automobile insurance. If you are a European citizen driving in Portugal in your own vehicle, bring along the International Motor Insurance Card, also known as the Green Insurance Card. It is issued by your insurance company in your home country and provides automobile insurance for you in Portugal.

As in all of continental Europe, cars are driven on the right side of the street. Seatbelt use is mandatory in the front and back seats, and

185

passengers under 13 years are not allowed in the front seat. Operating a cell telephone while driving is against the law. The speed limits are as follows, unless posted otherwise: 50 kmh (31 mph) in towns, 90 kmh (56 mph) on open highways outside town limits, and 120 kmh (75 mph) on freeways (*auto-estradas*). At intersections traffic coming from the right always has the right of way. Traffic circles (*rotundas*) are a new, albeit confusing attempt at regulating traffic at intersections, especially in smaller towns. Remember that those cars already in the circle always have the right of way. Since drunk driving is cause for innumerable accidents and deaths all over Portugal, the police take drunk driving as a serious offence. The legal blood alcohol level is 0.5 grams per liter, and depending on their blood alcohol level drivers can expect high fines and/or jail sentences for drunk driving offences.

General Guidelines

To drive safely on Portugal's roads there are several important factors you should keep in mind. The most important rule of the road in Portugal is to always expect the unexpected. Besides livestock returning from the pastures in the evening and slow agricultural machinery, watch out for narrow turns and potholes, especially on side roads and rural routes. On country roads, honk your horn before every narrow turn, and listen for the loud horns of buses and trucks. In case of an accident or breakdown dial 112 from any telephone, or, if on freeways, use the nearest orange emergency telephone. The Automóvel Clube de Portugal (Portuguese Automobile Club) provides 24-hour assistance in case of a breakdown.

There are 15 *auto-estradas* that connect Portugal's large cities. Portugal's freeways have largely been privatized, and a toll is charged on most sections. The IP or Itinerário Principal is a secondary divided highway and is usually toll-free. If you decide to drive in Portugal, make sure you get the latest available highway and city maps. Be aware of the chronic parking problem in most cities. Streets are narrow, and in most towns there are simply not enough parking spaces. Parked cars commonly block sidewalks, entrances, and alleys. It is not surprising that the *arrumador de carros*, the "car arranger", is a popular profession among the homeless and unemployed. These informal parking attendants point out available spots to drivers and help them drive up on the curb or behind a tree, and they are happy to get some change for their services.

Renting A Car

Renting a car is fairly easy and the requirements are similar to those in most other countries. Drivers need to be older than 21 years, and some rental agencies may require three years of driving experience. It is usually not necessary to show an international driver's license. All you need is your valid license from your home country, the international green insurance card from your home country (if you are a EU citizen), and a credit card or payment of a deposit. Most international rental car agencies such as Alamo, Avis, Budget, Europcar, Hertz, National, and Sixt have offices in Portugal, and there are also a number of smaller Portuguese rental agencies.

LAW ENFORCEMENT, CRIME, AND SAFETY

The Portuguese Police

The Guarda Nacional Republicana (GNR), the National Republican Guard, is responsible for maintaining order and security outside city limits. This includes patrolling highways and monitoring traffic, which is carried out by the Brigada de Trânsito, the traffic brigade which is a separate unit within the GNR. The Polícia de Segurança Pública (Public Security Police) is responsible for security and highway safety in urban areas and also conducts minor crime investigations. Although the police is in general friendly and helpful, incidents of police corruption and involvement in organized crime are allegedly on the rise. In general, however, foreigners have little to worry about regarding the police.

Drugs

Due to its strategic location, Portugal is a major entry point to the European market for drugs from all over the world. Since 2001, possession of small amounts of drugs and their consumption is merely an administrative offense (offenders are fined) and no longer a crime. Despite this tolerance toward drug use, the various police units are on alert at entry and exit points all across Portugal. Not a month goes by without a major drug bust. Be aware of drug dealers who approach you on the streets.

Crime and Safety

Although the crime rate is rising, Portugal is still a relatively safe country. As long as you take precautions and use common sense, you will be safe in Portugal. City centers, beaches, and tourist attractions are often frequented by pickpockets, and you should always keep an eye on your belongings. Be especially careful at railway stations, sidewalk cafes, and restaurants, on buses and subways, and in crowded places. Depending on where you live or plan to stay, it is a good idea to find out at the local tourist office about potentially dangerous parts of town. If you are ever victim of an assault, remain calm and do not attempt to attract attention. This may only frighten your assailants and put you in a dangerous situation. Hand over your belongings and leave the scene quickly. If you have your passport stolen, immediately report the incident to the nearest police station (*delegacia de polícia*) as well as to your consulate. To be able to cancel lost or stolen credit cards, keep account and contact information separate from your cards, and contact the credit card companies as soon as possible. Car break-ins are a regular occurrence in tourist areas, especially with rental cars and those with foreign license plates, so make sure that you do not leave valuables in your vehicle.

HEALTH CONSIDERATIONS

There is no need to take more health precautions than you normally would for any other European country. The best way to prepare yourself medically for a trip is to arrive in good health. Seeing a doctor in a foreign country can be a challenge, because of the language barrier and the uncertainty that comes with seeking medical help abroad. No special vaccinations are recommended for Portugal, but if you are concerned about food-borne illnesses you may want to consider a Hepatitis A vaccine. Depending on the length of your stay and your activity, you might consider a Hepatitis B and/or influenza vaccination as well. A few diseases are considered public health concerns in Portugal, among them hepatitis, tuberculosis, and mainly HIV/AIDS. In 2002, according to official data, there were approximately 21,000 reported cases of AIDS/HIV in Portugal, and there were 143 AIDS-related deaths. To reduce the risk of HIV infection, always use a condom during sexual intercourse and avoid sharing needles.

To help you get the right medical treatment if necessary, bring an international immunization record that lists all health conditions and allergies that you may have. If you take prescription medication, you should consider bringing a supply for the duration of your stay. Your other option is to see a local doctor to get a similar prescription, before you run out of medication. If you wear glasses or contact lenses, bring a spare pair or write down the prescription to be able to get a replacement easily. You should also consider bringing your favorite brands of non-prescription medications, since you might not be able to find them in Portugal.

Water from municipal water supplies is treated and does not pose a health risk. However, the water quality in rural areas often deteriorates during summer droughts. In this case you might prefer to buy bottled water or use a filtration system. Portugal has mild and pleasant weather, and foreigners usually don't have a lot of difficulties adjusting to Portugal's climate. Still, if you arrive in Portugal during the summer, be prepared to make adjustments to the heat, especially in the interior and the south. Give your body time to adjust to the different climate, especially if you spend a lot of time in the sun.

HEALTHCARE

Although Portugal still has lower health and human development indicators than most other EU countries, it has made great strides in the past few decades to improve health services and care for its citizens. As a result the life expectancy increased from 65 years in 1960 to 76 years in 2002. Infant mortality in 2002 was 5.84 per 1,000 live births.

The Healthcare System

It was not until the 1976 constitution that universal healthcare was introduced in Portugal with the creation of the National Health Service, the *Serviço Nacional de Saúde*. Although well-intended, the public healthcare system is today overburdened and underfunded, and barely capable of providing adequate healthcare for Portugal's citizens. Although Portugal has an adequate number of physicians, they are not evenly distributed throughout the country. Most doctors prefer to work in or near urban areas, and public health centers (*posto de saúde* or *centro de saúde*) in rural areas are often understaffed. With the public system inefficient and overburdened, those who can afford it get private health insurance, where they are able to get prompt treatment from private doctors and hospitals.

Seeking Medical Help

EU citizens can use the Portuguese healthcare system free of charge, as part of a reciprocal agreement among EU countries. They need to bring the form E 128 or E 111 with them to Portugal, which is issued by their local health board as proof of health insurance. Upon arrival in Portugal this document should be presented at the local health agency or health board, the *administração regional de saúde*, before seeking medical treatment.

If you are not a EU citizen or are not eligible for Portuguese health insurance through a job, you might want to consider other options. Find out if your health insurance at home covers health expenditures abroad, and if your provider will reimburse you for any medical treatment you paid for in Portugal. If this is not possible, it might be a good idea to sign up for a traveler's health insurance plan, which provides health coverage in case of medical emergencies. If you need medical attention while in Portugal, your consulate should be able to refer you to a reputable doctor or hospital. Keep in mind that you will probably have to pay for medical treatment and services at the time of the consultation, unless you have insurance in Portugal or elsewhere in the EU.

Emergencies

The *número nacional de socorro* (national emergency number) in Portugal is 112. This is a toll-free number that works everywhere in Portugal to call an ambulance, the police, or the fire department. In case of a medical emergency, you can either go to the *serviço de urgência* (emergency service) at the nearest hospital or dial 112.

Pharmacies

Pharmacies are usually open from 9:00am to 1:00pm and 3:00pm to 7:00pm from Monday to Friday and on Saturday mornings. Some of them are open late and on the weekend. After closing, most pharmacies put up a sign on the door indicating which nearby pharmacy has night or weekend service known as *farmácia de serviço*. If you have only a minor health concern you might consider just asking a pharmacist for assistance, instead of braving long waits at a public health center. On several occasions I was able to purchase prescription medication without a prescription, just by asking a pharmacist.

Hospitais (Hospitals)

Lisbon
Hospital de São Francisco Xavier
Estrada do Forte do Alto do Duque

tel: 21 300 03 00
http://www.hsfxavier.min-saude.pt

The British Hospital
Rua Saraiva de Carvalho, 49
tel: 21 394 31 00

Hospital de Santa Maria
Avenida Professor Egas Moniz
tel: 21 780 5333 or 21 780 5444
Urgência/emergency: 21 780 51 11 or 21 780 52 22
http://www.hsm.pt

Porto
Hospital Geral de Santo António
Largo Professor Abel Salazar
tel: 22 207 75 00
Hospital de São João
Alameda Professor Hernâni Monteiro
tel: 22 551 21 00

Algarve
Hospital Distrital de Faro
Rua Leão Penedo
tel 28 989 11 00

Hospital Particular do Algarve
Estrada de Alvor, Lote 27
Cruz Bota, Alvor-Portimão
tel: 28 242 04 00

EDUCATION

During most of Portugal's history education was a privilege of the nobility and clergy.

It was not until after the 1974 revolution that basic education was extended to include a larger percentage of the population. Three decades after the fall of the dictatorship the education level of the Portuguese remains low. Over a third of the population only attended school for four years, and another third did not get past the mandatory nine years. Only 8.6% of the population has a university degree. Portugal's illiteracy rate (age 10 and over) was 9% in 2001, the highest in the EU.

Basic Education

The Portuguese education system is divided into several stages. The *ensino básico* (basic education) lasts for nine years (ages 6–15) and is mandatory. It consists of the *primeiro ciclo* (first cycle) with four years (ages 6–10), the *segundo ciclo* (second cycle) with two years

University students in their traditional suits.

193

(ages 11–12), and the *terceiro ciclo* (third cycle), which lasts for three years (ages 13–15). After completing the mandatory *ensino básico*, attendance at the *escola secundária* (secondary school) is voluntary and takes three years (ages 16–18). After that, students have the option of attending university or a variety of technical colleges.

Higher Education

Throughout most of Portugal's history the university of Coimbra was the country's only academic institution. Portugal's university system was only extended in the early 20th century, when the universities of Lisbon and Porto were founded. During the 1970s, a number of small universities were founded in several other cities. In addition to these public universities there are numerous private universities and institutes (known as *Instituto Superior* or *Escola Superior*) offering both vocational and academic fields of study. To study at a university, Portuguese students need to pass an entrance exam, and the number of spaces are limited depending on the chosen discipline and the number of applicants. The academic year runs from September/October through May, with a summer vacation from June to September.

Chapter Thirteen

WORK AND BUSINESS

"Se queres ter boa fama, não te tome o sol na cama."
(If you want to achieve fame, don't let the sun surprise you
in bed.)

—Portuguese proverb

WORKING IN PORTUGAL

Legal Requirements and Considerations

EU citizens can work in Portugal without a work permit or visa, but
they still need to legalize their status by getting a tax number,
registering with social security, and signing a work contract. Until
recently, it was quite easy for citizens of countries outside the EU to

come to Portugal as a tourist, find a job, and get a work authorization locally. This is no longer the case, since Portugal has recently begun to close its doors to immigrants as part of a process to establish a common EU immigration policy. It is also no longer possible for illegal immigrants to legalize or change their immigration status while in Portugal, and anybody without legal status in Portugal is now obliged to leave. The new law also provides for high fines for companies that hire illegal immigrants. Foreign citizens from outside the EU can apply for a temporary residency visa (*autorização de permanência*) at a Portuguese consulate, provided they have a work offer or a signed work contract, have not committed any serious crimes, and have not been previously deported. Portuguese consulates provide information about jobs and employment opportunities for those who do not already have a job offer or signed contract. The immigrant quota is established every year by the government in accordance with the labor unions, trade organizations, and the needs of the labor market.

Finding Work

Portugal has one of the lowest salary levels in Europe, which is why few Western Europeans seek employment in Portugal. Most foreigners working in Portugal are immigrants from Brazil or from poor African or Eastern European countries, and the large majority of them work in the service sector and in construction. Most of the citizens of developed countries who work in Portugal are either employed by embassies and multinational corporations in highly qualified professions, or they own businesses. International students who spend a semester or a year at a Portuguese university often seek part-time employment at bars or other odd jobs, but the pay is very low. Students and other young foreigners often find work at bars and restaurants in Lisbon's Bairro Alto, or on the Algarve coast, where knowledge of Portuguese is not a primary requirement. If you have qualifications to teach English and are able to work legally, contact language schools and ask around. Check the local Yellow Pages (*páginas amarelas*) under *escolas* (schools). You can also check the employment section of newspaper classifieds for *aulas de Inglês* (English classes) or *ensino* (instruction).

In addition to bars and restaurants there is also a considerable informal employment market in the service industry and construction trade, mostly in low-paying positions. But the tough new immigration laws make it more difficult for foreigners without work permits to find employment. Keep in mind that informal work also poses several risks. For one thing, there is no record of your employment, and if you don't get paid, you can't do anything about it. Secondly, you are not covered in case of a work-related accident, and do not make contributions for unemployment coverage or health care. In case of an informal work situation, it may be a good idea to request payment daily to make sure you are compensated for your work. Also, if you are from a country outside the EU, you may be subject to deportation if you are caught working in Portugal illegally.

Employee Rights and Benefits

If you work in Portugal, you are protected by Portuguese laws regulating the rights and obligations of employees. Salaries are regulated by collective labor treaties and follow strict guidelines. Portuguese labor law and constitution prohibits dismissal without a just cause. In 2003, the minimum wage was 365.60 euros per month, which is adjusted annually for inflation. The Portuguese labor code proposes a workweek of 40 hours, which can be modified by collective labor agreements. There are strict laws regulating overtime. Employees are entitled to paid holidays, currently 13 national holidays and 1 local holiday, in addition to 22 days of paid vacation per calendar year. Every employee is also entitled a bonus of two extra monthly salaries per year, usually paid in August and December.

Income Tax and Other Withholdings

There are two so-called direct taxes (taxed at the source) in Portugal: the corporate income tax (*imposto sobre as rendas de pessoas colectivas*, IRC) and the individual income tax (*imposto sobre as rendas de pessoas singulares,* IRS). For individuals there are six different income tax brackets depending on income. The tax rate varies from 12% to a maximum of 40% for residents of Portugal. For non-residents the income tax rate is set at 25%. Under Portuguese law you are considered a resident for tax purposes if you live in Portugal for at least 183 days per year. As a non-resident you are only taxed on income earned in Portugal. As a resident of Portugal you are supposed to declare worldwide income. Keep in mind that many countries require tax payments on worldwide income, and you may owe tax in your home country on income earned in Portugal. Make sure you find out about any tax treaties between Portugal and your home country to avoid double taxation. Portugal currently has double taxation treaties with all EU countries and many other countries worldwide.

In addition to income tax, employees also make a monthly contribution to social security (*segurança social*), which are withheld automatically. For most employees the social security tax is approximately 34.75% of the gross income, of which 11% is paid by the employee and 23.75% by the employer. The social security tax includes contributions for healthcare, unemployment, sickness benefits, and retirement. The legal retirement age is 65 years, a few years less for public employees. Portugal has reciprocal social security agreements with several countries, and it is worth finding out if your home country is among them. Employees are also entitled to unemployment coverage and sick leave. Mothers are entitled to three months of paid maternity leave.

DOING BUSINESS IN PORTUGAL

"To do business in our country, it is indispensable to

conquer the sympathy of the buyer."
—Jorge Dias, *Os Elementos Fundamentais da Cultura
Portuguesa*, 1955

Portugal is a very traditional country, and when doing business there keep in mind that business practices and methods may not follow the latest trends. In Portugal business deals depend a whole lot on personal relations and connections, and not so much on pushy or sly business tactics or offers to "cut a deal." You are in a small country where it is important to get to know the business community and use effective networking techniques. The question may not be what great deal you can offer that one time, but how and if you can be integrated as a reliable and long-term member of the local business community. It is important to emphasize your sincerity and your commitment to doing long-term business in Portugal.

When doing business in Portugal, be aware that the Portuguese are patriotic and have a strong sense of pride, which makes them skeptical and cautious when dealing with foreigners. The degree of foreign presence and investment in business is a polemic topic that is constantly discussed. It comes down to the fact that the Portuguese are not entirely comfortable with relinquishing economic control of their country to companies from abroad. The Portuguese realize that they need foreign investment to stimulate the economy and create jobs, but at the same time they are deeply ambivalent about selling off their economy and in a wider sense their national sovereignty. European integration has been completely achieved on paper, but it will take a few more years before the Portuguese will be entirely comfortable with the presence of foreign companies. This caution is also reflected in the fact that the government still retains golden shares of privatized sectors that were sold to foreign interests.

A Traditional Economy

Portugal's economy is still predominantly based on traditional sectors (commerce, trade, light manufacturing), which produce most of the wealth and employ most of the workers. Portugal's business landscape is characterized by a large number of small businesses with only a few employees, especially in the services and commerce sectors. Modern service sectors such as communications and financial services are gaining importance but still have not achieved a dominant status in the economy. Small high-tech companies have emerged as Portugal's most dynamic economic sector in recent years, but by EU standards Portugal invests very little in research and development, which stifles growth in high-tech sectors such as information technology.

Infrastructure and Modernization

Thanks to EU development funds, Portugal has been able to significantly modernize its infrastructure since joining the EC in 1986. New highways were built, ports were upgraded, the telecommunications system was modernized, and hydroelectric capacity was expanded. But despite decades of community aid, Portugal has experienced a highly unequal regional development. Most development programs benefited Portugal's economic centers, leaving interior regions largely unaffected by modernization and infrastructure improvements. Little has been done to revive the economies of remote regions and combat the excessive migration of the past decades.

Privatizations and Foreign Investment

Throughout the 1990s, an ambitious privatization program raised large revenues for the Portuguese government, amounting to several billion dollars each year. Privatization also raised productivity and quality of service, and Portugal's economy became much more dynamic, flexible, and competitive. Telecommunications, finance, transportation, energy, and other vital economic sectors and industries are now largely owned by the private sector, although the government still maintains golden shares in some key sectors. In 2002, foreign direct investment into Portugal totaled US$4.3 billion, a clear sign that companies are attracted by the incentive packages offered by the government as well as by Portugal's low labor costs. Numerous large multinational companies, mainly from the electronics and automobile sector, have invested in Portugal over the past decade and take advantage of Portugal's strategic location for overseas exports.

Productivity

While Salazar kept the public sector small, it experienced substantial growth after the 1974 revolution, mainly because of the nationalization of key industries and the creation of many new government agencies. The growing public sector also became a way for political parties to secure votes by offering workers stable employment and benefits in public administration. Privatization improved the productivity in many economic sectors, and modern principles of market economics were applied to make companies more competitive on the international marketplace. The public sector, on the other hand, remains inefficient and over-inflated and is in urgent need of structural reforms. Portugal's

labor productivity is among the lowest in the EU, mainly due to its large public sector of 700,000 employees, which accounts for an astronomical 15% of Portugal's GDP. Numerous analyses have pointed out that unless Portugal carries out structural reforms in the unproductive public sector and manages to increase the overall productivity of the work force, it will not be able to reach the desired high growth figures that were the hallmark of the Portuguese economy in the late 1980s and 1990s.

Labor Market

One of the main challenges to the Portuguese economy is the low level of qualification of its workforce, among the lowest in the EU. Several studies have shown that Portugal's education system significantly lags behind the demands of the market economy and that the government does not invest enough in the training and education of workers. This fact has been recognized as one of the major obstacles to improving Portugal's productivity and stimulating economic growth, since qualified personnel in dynamic sectors is hard to find. Portugal's labor market is also characterized by a strong concentration in the major cities. Most workers move to cities for better paying jobs, and few qualified people remain in the interior regions, where adequate human resources are lacking to attract new businesses. The few large companies in the interior mostly operate in sectors that require little qualification, such as textiles and light industry. In order to attract diverse and modern companies to impoverished and depopulated regions, it will be necessary to improve the qualifications of workers and attract people with a higher education.

Labor Unions

Legalized after the 1974 revolution, labor unions are still a strong force to reckon with in Portugal's labor disputes, especially since they have the sole right to collective contract negotiations. Strikes are fairly common in Portugal, and rarely a month goes by without one of the major unions calling for a strike in one economic sector or another. One week it may be the garbage collectors, the next week the railway employees, and the following week it may be the doctors. Portugal's largest and most influential unions are the communist-controlled *Confederação Geral dos Trabalhadores Portugueses* (General Confederation of Portuguese Workers), and the socialist *União Geral dos Trabalhadores* (General Workers' Union).

Corruption and Other Ills

Portugal has traditionally been lax about prosecuting white-collar crime. But in recent years, the country has been fraught with so many high-level corruption scandals that the justice system can no longer turn a deaf ear to this serious problem. Payoff and kickback schemes have involved politicians, highly respected citizens, and even such popular heroes as soccer team presidents. Tax evasion, at which the Portuguese are considered experts, is another offense that until recently has been largely overlooked. Only Portugal's growing budget deficit has made it necessary for the finance department to wield its strong arm and threaten companies and individuals with high fines, unless they paid the back-owed taxes and social security payments. Around Christmas 2002, an appeal to the Portuguese by Lisbon's Catholic patriarch to "give to the emperor the things that are the emperor's" resulted in such a rush to the tax offices to pay up owed taxes, that the tax revenue during the last days of 2002 was large enough to save the budget deficit from exceeding the 3% limit set by the EU.

In a country were family ties are strong, it is not surprising that nepotism and cronyism are also long-standing traditions. These practices probably go back to the monarchy, when a few influential families divided up the best government jobs among themselves. This kinship system was historically of great importance in Portugal and on a smaller scale still plays a role in public and economic life today. Such networks of close personal connections, be it of relatives,

friends, or peers from a shared social, political, or academic background, are based on mutual assistance, favors, and obligations and are used to yield political influence as well as to promote business and enhance career opportunities. Even today, whenever there is a change in local government, many important administrative positions are given to relatives and cronies.

Clearing Bureaucratic Hurdles

Complicated laws and regulations together with the bureaucratic inflexibility of an oversized public sector have turned Portugal's public institutions into inefficient behemoths, incapable of dealing with important matters in a timely matter. From the backlogged justice system, to getting permits, or simply requesting information, foreigners will find the inefficiency of Portugal's bureaucracy almost unbearable. Fortunately, for those with little patience and time to go through the bureaucratic drudgery themselves, there are agents known as *despachantes* who specialize in cutting through the red tape of Portugal's government agencies. These professionals are familiar with most legal proceedings, forms, and requirements and will help you get things done quickly and effectively. They can help you with getting a business permit, a property title, or just about any other document or license you may need. *Despachantes* can be especially helpful for those new to Portugal who don't know how to deal with all the red tape regarding their residency papers and other legal matters. If in need of a *despachante,* contact the local expatriate community, your consulate, or your country's foreign trade office for a list of recommended agents.

BUSINESS ETIQUETTE AND STYLE

Establishing Contacts

There are numerous ways to make business contacts in Portugal. If there is a foreign trade office of your country in Portugal, you already have a great advantage. You can contact them beforehand and get information about potential business partners and the local business environment. The Resource Guide at the end of this book lists several institutions that might be helpful to you. You should also contact the Portuguese consulate in your country and get information. There may also be an office of ICEP (Investment, Commerce and Tourism or *Investimento, Comércio e Turismo*) in your country, which is the Portuguese government agency that promotes Portugal to international businesses and investors. Your consulate in Portugal might also be able to help you establish business contacts and provide you with further information. Remember that many business deals are made through personal connections, and that it is important to establish personal relations with potential partners or clients.

If you come to Portugal on business, you will most likely make business contacts in one of the few large cities such as Porto or Lisbon. Most likely the businesses you will deal with have already worked with foreign companies before and have a certain degree of knowledge about international business style and practices. Unless you speak Portuguese well or know that your negotiation partners speak excellent English, it is best to hire an interpreter, or make arrangements with your negotiation partners for translation service. It may also be a good idea to have documents translated into Portuguese to facilitate negotiations. But regardless of the language of negotiation, it is still a good idea to learn some Portuguese before coming to Portugal. Knowing a few phrases and being able to use common greetings will certainly make a positive impression. Depending on the nature of your business interests in Portugal (long-term or short-term), it may be worth reading a few books about Portuguese culture to gain a better understanding of the culture and the people.

Meeting for Business

At the beginning of a meeting it is customary to shake hands with everyone present. People also shake hands at the end of a business meeting. The handshake is firm and people look each other in the eye. Introductions at business meetings are formal, stating the first and last name, function, and title. As a general guideline, a person lower in rank is introduced to the superior, a younger person to the older and a man to a woman. It is common to exchange business cards (*cartão de visita*) during meetings or when making a contact, so make sure you bring a sufficient supply with you.

In Portugal, conducting business is based on establishing personal relationships. Therefore, expect business meetings to begin with a casual conversation, where you may be offered a refreshment or coffee.

You will doubtlessly leave a better impression in conversation if your statements about Portugal reflect current events and if you demonstrate a certain knowledge and insight about Portugal. Even knowing about the latest successes (presumably) of the Portuguese soccer team, can help you in informal conversations. Personal topics such as family life are avoided during such conversations, unless the participants know each other well. Family matters and personal questions are a very private affair to the Portuguese. In general, go with the flow of the conversation and follow the lead of your Portuguese conversation partners. If you are part of a foreign delegation in Portugal, expect your hosts or business contacts to provide for some entertainment. This could be a dinner invitation to a typical restaurant, or an invitation to a concert, theater, or ballet. Some tourist activities may also be included, or you may be invited to play golf.

Business Lunch

Business lunches are a great opportunity to make a first business contact with a representative of a company you would like to do business with or someone who interests you as a potential business partner. A business lunch is usually held at a good restaurant, and the inviting party picks the restaurant and pays the bill. As a general rule, formal table etiquette should be observed during business lunches. During the meal the conversation is usually pleasant and informal. Avoid topics such as politics, which might lead to extended discussions and offend people. A business lunch has the primary purpose of establishing contacts and to socialize. Business matters are usually not discussed until the end of the meal, around the time when coffee is served. It is usually the host who brings up the topic of business first.

In addition to business lunches there are several other ways for business partners or clients to socialize and talk business informally. Such an occasion could be a breakfast meeting at a hotel, or meeting for a coffee or cocktail at a bar in the afternoon, or even a dinner at a restaurant, although dinners are generally considered part of family life. Remember that the primary purpose is to establish contacts and to keep in touch, not to close business deals. If agreements are made during such a conversation, it is customary to work out the details at a proper business meeting at a later time.

Punctuality

> *"Amanhã é outro dia."*
> (Tomorrow is another day.)
>
> —Portuguese saying

207

The Portuguese are much more relaxed about timeliness than northern Europeans or North Americans. The Anglo-American attitude of "Time is money" is not valid here, and it is common for the Portuguese to arrive 15 to 30 minutes late for appointments and meetings. Especially the public sector is very relaxed about punctuality, and opening hours should not be taken too seriously. Nonetheless, as a foreigner, your professionalism reflects on the reputation and credibility of your company, and it is best to arrive on time.

Women In Business

Women in Portugal are only just beginning to climb the corporate ladder, and only on rare occasions will you find a woman in a higher position. Many Portuguese men still see women as belonging in the home, and women may not always receive the same respect as men in the business world. When dealing with a Portuguese woman in a business setting, make sure you extend all the courtesy that a lady expects in Portugal. Open the door for her, help her take off and put on her coat, and help her with the chair when sitting down. On the other hand, as a foreign woman on business in Portugal, it is best to accept the courtesies extended to you by Portuguese men. You may not share the Portuguese penchant for chivalric traditions and may find the attention from men a little patronizing, but it is best to accept these situations as "cultural experiences" and not react with consternation, especially in business situations.

Dressing for Business and Work

How to dress for business depends on the type of business and the occasion. The Portuguese business environment is status-conscious and traditional. The better dressed you are for business, the more seriously you will be taken. In case of doubt it is better to overdress, as to shed no doubt on your professionalism and credibility. Women dress elegantly although discreetly. They should avoid bright colors, provocative clothing (such as tight-fitting dresses or mini skirts) as well as jeans, high heels, and strong perfumes. Women use light make-up and do not wear excessive jewelry to work. Men usually wear a suit and tie, and in less formal work environments they can get away with slacks and a jacket or just a shirt.

Chapter Fourteen

OVERCOMING THE LANGUAGE BARRIER

A language is a place where one sees the world,
And in which are drawn the limits of our thoughts
and feelings.
From my language one sees the sea.
From my language one hears its roar,
as from others one would hear the forest,
or the silence of the desert.
That's why the voice of the sea was the voice
of our restlessness.

   —from the poem *Conta Corrente* by Vergílio Ferreira

THE LANGUAGE CHALLENGE

I once told a friend that I spoke both Spanish and Portuguese. She looked at me in surprise and said: "Isn't that cheating? Isn't Portuguese just like Spanish?" Her statement sums up what many people think about the difference between these two languages. But nothing could be further from the truth. Although similar to Spanish in its written form, Portuguese sounds very different. In fact, it is not easy to recognize spoken Portuguese as a Romance language, and many people have compared its sound to Russian. Luckily for Spanish-speakers, written Portuguese resembles Spanish enough that the meaning of a text can be understood. To speak the language well and to understand the Portuguese in conversation, however, takes some practice and study.

Probably the best way to make your stay in Portugal more enjoyable is to learn the language. To get a grasp on this difficult language it is important to start a language course before you get to Portugal. The sooner you start with a course at home, the sooner you will master the essentials of basic conversation after your arrival. Language is not merely a form of communication, it is the key to a deeper understanding of a foreign culture. With a basic vocabulary you begin to understand colloquial expressions and get an insider's look at an interesting culture and a friendly people. The most important step toward overcoming the language barrier is to start practicing. Bring a phrase book and dictionary and start building an active vocabulary. Write down words you don't know so you can look them up later, and don't hesitate to ask people about the meaning of words and phrases.

If you decide to study Portuguese by yourself keep in mind that European Portuguese varies significantly in pronunciation from the Portuguese spoken in Brazil. If available, purchase a course that teaches European Portuguese, so you won't have to relearn the pronunciation and various grammatical differences. For a list of self-study courses and Portuguese language schools in Portugal see the Resource Guide at the end of this book.

INTRODUCTION TO EUROPEAN PORTUGUESE

Portuguese is the world's sixth most popular language and is spoken by over 200 million people on four continents. It is the official language in eight countries: Portugal, Brazil, Cabo Verde, Angola, Mozambique, Guinea Bissau, São Tomé and Príncipe, and most recently East Timor. The Portuguese in all of these countries has slight variations, with Brazilian Portuguese being the most different, not only in pronunciation, but also in grammar and syntax.

Portuguese is part of the Romance language family of Indo-European languages, together with Spanish, French, Italian, and Romanian. Just like Spanish, Portuguese developed from a local dialect of vulgar Latin that had evolved in the centuries following the Roman occupation. The long Moorish occupation of Portugal also left its traces in the language, and there are still many words of Arabic origins in the modern Portuguese vocabulary, such as *alfândega* (customs building), *chafariz* (fountain), *aceite* (olive oil), *garrafa* (bottle), *xarope* (syrup), and many others.

PRONUNCIATION

The main challenge of Portuguese pronunciation for English speakers are the characteristic nasal sounds. Most other phonemes are similar to those in English. In the phonetic transcriptions of Portuguese words in the section below I have used capital letters to indicate stress. This introduction is only a rough guideline to the pronunciation of European Portuguese. It is best to buy a language course with a cassette or CD to learn the correct pronunciation. Make sure you get a program that teaches European Portuguese.

Vowels

In European Portuguese, the vowels are often silent, swallowed, or not stressed, which sometimes gives the impression that Portuguese just consists of consonants. To many foreigners the word *Portugal* therefore sounds more like *Prtu-gl*. The following list is only a general guideline, since the pronunciation varies with regional dialects:

A is pronounced as the **u** in s**u**n or the a in f**a**ther, e.g. *alarmante* (alarming) is pronounced "a-lar-MAHN-te."

E can be open like the **e** in **e**gg, e.g. *dez* (ten) is pronounced "dezh", or closed like the **a** in st**a**te, e.g. *seco* (dry) is pronounced "SAY-co". When written with an acute accent, the **é** takes the stress and becomes an open vowel, e.g. *café* (coffee) is pronounced "ka-FEH". With a circumflex **ê** also takes the stress, but is a closed vowel as in *três* (three), which is pronounced "tresh". At the end of a word, **e** is often swallowed and therefore silent, e.g. *saudade* (nostalgic longing) is pronounced "soh-DAHD".

EI mostly appears in the middle of a word and is pronounced somewhere between st**ay** and f**ly**, e.g. *beira* (edge, shore) is pronounced "BAY-ra".

I is pronounced as the **i** in **i**diom or **ee**l, e.g. *idioma* (language) is pronounced "ee-dee-OH-ma"; with an acute accent **í** takes the stress, e.g. *magnífico* (magnificent) is pronounced "ma-GNEE-fee-co".

O is mainly pronounced open as the **o** in c**o**d, e.g. *nove* (nine) is pronounced "NO-ve" or closed, similar to the **o** in b**o**at, e.g. *motor* (motor) is pronounced "mo-TOR". The definite article **o** (the) is a short vowel that sounds more like the **u** in p**u**t. At the end of a word, **o** is often swallowed and silent. With an acute accent, **ó** takes the stress with an open pronunciation, e.g. *avó* (grandmother) which is pronounced "a-VAW". When written with a circumflex, **ô** takes the stress and becomes a closed vowel, e.g. *avô* (grandfather), which is pronounced "a-VOH".

OU is closed like the **o** in s**o**, e.g. *outro* (other) is pronounced "OH-tro".

U is either a long vowel as in b**oo**t, e.g. *burro* (donkey) is pronounced "BOOR-ro", or a short vowel as in p**u**t, e.g. *sucursal* (branch office) is pronounced "su-kur-SAL". **U** is silent in words with **qu** and **gu** when followed by **e** or **i**, e.g. *quebrar* (to break) is pronounced "ke-BRAR" and *seguir* (to follow) is pronounced "se-

GEAR". U is written as **ü** after **g** or **q** and before **e** or **i**, only when it needs to be pronounced. In this position, **u** sounds more like a **w**, e.g. *agüentar* (to tolerate) is pronounced "a-gwen-TAR" and *freqüente* (frequent) is pronounced "fre-KWENT". When **u** follows a **g** or **q** and precedes an **a**, it also sounds more like a **w**, e.g. *guarda* (guard) is pronounced "GWAR-da" and *quando* (when) is pronounced "KWAHN-do".

Nasal Diphthongs

Ã and **ãs** are a nasal **ah** sound, e.g. *irmã* (sister) is pronounced "eer-MAH", and *irmãs* (sisters) is "eer-MAHSH".

Ãe and **ães** are a nasal **eye** sound, e.g. *mãe* (mother) is pronounced "my" and *cães* (dogs) is "kysh".

Am, **ão**, and **ãos** are a nasal **ow** sound, e.g. *olham* (they look) is pronounced "OHL-yow", *irmão* (brother) is "eer-MOW", and *irmãos* (brothers) is "eer-MOWSH".

Em and **ens** are a nasal **ay** sound, e.g. *homem* (man) is pronounced "OH-may" and *parabéns* (congratulations) is "pa-ra-BAYSH".

Im, **in** and **ins** are a nasal **ee** sound, e.g. *amendoim* (peanut) is pronounced "a-men-do-EEM" and *rins* (kidneys) is "REENSH".

Om and **ons** are a nasal **o** sound as in the French *bon*, e.g. *bom* (good) is pronounced "bo" and *sons* (sounds) is "sosh".

Ões is a nasal **oys** sound, e.g. *botões* (buttons) is pronounced "bo-TOYSH".

Um and **uns** are a nasal **oo** sound, e.g. *um* (one) is pronounced "oom" and *alguns* (some) is "al-GOONSH".

Consonants

B, F, P, V are generally pronounced as in English.

C – as in **c**at, e.g. *caro* (expensive) is pronounced "CAH-ro". When followed by **e** or **i**, it is pronounced as in **c**ent, e.g. *cedo* (early) is pronounced "CEH-do" and *cinto* (belt) is "CIN-to".

Ç – as in **s**it, e.g. *aço* (steel) is pronounced "AH-so".

CH – as in **sh**oe, e.g. *chave* (key) is pronounced "SHAH-ve".

D – as in English, e.g. *diz* (he/she says) is pronounced "deezh".

G – as the **g** in **g**oal, e.g. *galo* (cock) is pronounced "GAH-lo". When followed by **e** or **i**, the **g** becomes a melodious **sh** as in pleasure, e.g. *gengibre* (ginger) is pronounced "zhen-ZHEE-bre".

H – always silent as in **h**erb, e.g. *hotel* is pronounced "oh-TEL".

J – a melodious **sh** as in pleasure, e.g. *jeropiga* (a liqueur wine) is pronounced "zhe-ro-PEE-ga".

K – not part of the Portuguese alphabet, but is used in adopted foreign words such as **k**etchup. It is pronounced just as the English **k** in **k**ind.

L – as in English, e.g. Portugal is pronounced "Por-tu-GAL".

LH – as in million, e.g. *alho* (garlic) is pronounced "AHL-yo".

M – as in English, e.g. *mar* (sea) is pronounced "mar". **M** is silent when part of a nasal diphthong. See above.

N – as in English, e.g. *nata* (cream) is pronounced "NAH-ta". **N** is silent when part of a nasal diphthong. See above.

NH – a nasal sound pronounced as the **n** in on**i**on, e.g. *ninho* (nest) is pronounced "NEEN-yo".

QU – pronounced as **k** when followed by **e** or **i**, e.g. *questão* (question) is pronounced "kes-TOW" and *quilômetro* (kilometer) is "kee-LOH-me-tro". When followed by **a** or **o**, it is pronounced as the **qu** in **qu**estion, e.g. *quando* (when) is pronounced "KWAHN-do".

R – in northern Portugal, **r** is rolled the way it is in Spanish while in the Lisbon area, it is pronounced as a guttural sound like in French, e.g. *rato* (mouse) is pronounced "RAH-to". The same pronunciation applies to **rr**, e.g. *carro* (car) is pronounced "KAR-ro".

S – as in **s**it at the beginning of a word, e.g. *sapo* (frog) is pronounced "SAH-po". In the middle of a word, **s** is pronounced as the **sh** in **sh**y when followed by a consonant, e.g. *destruir* (to destroy) is pronounced "desh-troo-EER". At the end of a word, **s** is mostly pronounced as the **sh** in **sh**oe, e.g. *barcos* (boats) is pronounced

"BAR-cosh". **Ss** is pronounced as the **s** in s**i**t, e.g. *nosso* (our) is pronounced "NOS-so".

T – as in English, e.g. *tia* (aunt) is pronounced "TEE-a".

W – does not exist in the Portuguese language, although it occasionally appears in foreign words. It is pronounced like the English **w**, e.g. *Walter* is pronounced "WAL-ter".

X – pronounced in several different ways. At the beginning of a word, **x** is always pronounced as the **sh** in sh**o**e, e.g. **x**ale (shawl) is pronounced "SHAH-le". In the middle of a word, **x** is also pronounced as the **sh** in **sh**oe, e.g. *explorar* (to explore) is pronounced "esh-ploh-RAR", except in the combination **ex** before a vowel, when it is pronounced as the **z** in ma**z**e, e.g. *exemplo* (example) is pronounced "e-ZEM-plo". In foreign adopted words, **x** is pronounced as in English, e.g. *fax* is pronounced "FAHX" and *táxi* is "TAK-see".

Y – does not exist in the Portuguese language, but it occasionally appears in adapted foreign names. It is pronounced as the **y** in Jud**y**.

Z – pronounced as the **z** in ma**z**e when it appears at the beginning and in the middle of a word, e.g. *zero* (zero) is pronounced "ZEH-ro" and *prazer* (pleasure) is "pra-ZER". At the end of a word, **z** becomes a melodious **sh** as in plea**s**ure, e.g. *feliz* (happy) is pronounced "feh-LEEZH".

Stress

As a general rule, stress falls on the next-to-last syllable, when a word ends in the vowels **a, e,** or **o,** and the consonants **m** and **s**:

alegre (joyful) – "a-LEH-gre";
perto (close) – "PER-to";
homem (man) – "OH-may";
serviços (services) – "ser-VEE-sosh".

All other words have the stress on the last syllable:
comer (eat) – "ko-MER";
quintal (backyard) – "kin-TAL";

capaz (capable) – "ca-PAZH".

Exceptions:
A syllable with an accent or a tilde always takes the stress:
alfândega (custom house) – "al-FAN-de-gah";
pérola (pearl) – "PER-o-la";
responsável (responsible) – "res-pon-SAH-vel";
polícia (police) – "po-LEE-se-a";
irmão (brother) – "eer-MAO";
alemães (Germans) – "a-le-MAH-esh";
sermões (sermons) – "ser-MOH-esh".

There are several other exceptions that follow special rules.

EVERYDAY PORTUGUESE

Dialects, Slang, and Colloquial Expressions
Portugal has a number of dialects that characterize the various regions. There is, for example, a noticeable difference in pronunciation between someone from Trás-os-Montes and the Alentejo region. There are also various forms of slang, known as *calão*, that are used by different social circles or professions. University students have their own *calão*, and so do fishermen and farmers. Here are just a few terms that are popular with young people and college students:

giro – great, fabulous
fixe – great, cool,
à maneira – great, cool
gajo – guy, fellow

Portuguese is also rich in colloquial expressions, some of which are very metaphorical and amusing:
Falar pelos cotovelos: It literally means "to talk by the elbows," and is used to describe someone who talks a lot.

Ficar tudo em águas de bacalhau: This is one of the most typical Portuguese expressions. It literally means "it all stays in codfish water," that is, it all ends up in nothing or results in nothing.

Meter a viola no saco: It literally means "to put the *viola* in the bag," and refers to the act of keeping quiet about something.

Pescadinha de rabo na boca: It literally means "a hake with the tail in its mouth," as a metaphor for a vicious cycle or paradoxical situation.

Exclamations and Curses

Portuguese very rarely curse, and proper language and behavior are very important in public. The list below is less intended as a working vocabulary than to clarify the meaning of a few of the most common curse words and interjections.

credo! – expression of disbelief

meu Deus! – oh my God!

se Deus quiser! – God willing!

pá! – widely used exclamation of surprise, disbelief, or encouragement

ai! ui! – expression of pain or surprise

fogo! – expression of enthusiasm, appreciation, and surprise

Força! – exclamation of encouragement

caramba! – darn!

Proverbial Wisdom

Portuguese proverbs are an important form of cultural expression, especially those proverbs that are uniquely Portuguese and do not have the same version in another language. These proverbs reflect Portugal's unique cultural context and contain interesting references to daily life or traditional activities.

Azeitona e a fortuna, às vezes muita e às vezes nenhuma

It literally means "olive oil and good fortune, at times a lot and at times none at all." This is a very poignant comparison of good luck with the olive harvest: it is unpredictable, some years the harvest can be rich, in other years very poor.

Para quem é bacalhau, basta

It literally means "it is good enough for a codfish." Cod was considered the low-quality food of the poor for a long time and its former reputation lives on in proverbs. This proverb refers to someone who is simple and not very distinguished, just like codfish, and who is not very demanding and easily satisfied with something of low quality.

Falar aos peixes

It literally means "to speak to the fish." This proverb suggests that someone is talking to deaf ears. It refers to a miracle known as the "sermon to the fish" affected by St. Anthony of Pádua, a Portuguese-born saint. In this legend, the saint told an inattentive crowd in Italy's Rimini that even fish were better listeners. He then walked down to the river and when he began to preach, all the fish lifted their heads out of the water to listen to St. Anthony's sermon.

GESTURES AND SIGNS

The Portuguese are formal and somewhat restrained in public and do not gesticulate or use much body language in conversation. They also rarely use offensive gestures, for the same reason that they do not curse in public: good manners are an important indicator of status. But gestures are still sometimes used to emphasize what is being said or to attract someone's attention. A more lively body language is used in informal social settings and in the presence of friends and family. This is when people frequently touch each other on the arm or shoulder during a conversation. Below I have listed several common gestures. As you become more familiar with the culture and meet more people, you will doubtlessly discover several more.

Attracting Attention

To get someone's attention, the Portuguese raise their arm, palm facing forward, and make a waving motion by wagging their fingers up and down.

Hand Brush

Hold your hands in front of your body, the palms facing you. With one hand brush over the outside of the other hand, then repeat this gesture with the other hand. This means that you couldn't care less or that something doesn't bother or interest you.

The Obscene O

Known in North America as the *okay* sign, this gesture of the index finger and thumb forming an "o" is an insult in Portugal.

Thumbs Up

This gesture signifies that something is going well or that something is okay or fine. One hand forms a fist and the thumb is pointed straight up. It resembles the American "thumbs up" gesture, but is executed with only one hand. Do not use the American 'okay' sign instead, which is an insult.

Expensive

When people express that something is expensive, they hold out their hand, and rub the straight index and middle fingers against the thumb several times, as if handling money.

Pinching An Earlobe

When people talk about a delicious meal or food item, they pinch an earlobe with their thumb and index finger.

CULTURAL QUIZ

SITUATION ONE

You are on one of Portugal's magnificent small beaches and would like a late afternoon refreshment. When you walk up to the only beachside bar and are about to sit down at a table, you realize that the bartender is immersed in a game of cards with her friends at one of the outdoor tables. Instead of sitting down, you decide to walk up to the counter to attract her attention. Even though you are sure the waitress must have taken notice of your arrival by now, she ignores you and continues with her game. You walk back and forth along the counter, clear your throat, and look at her from a distance—to no avail. Only after the game of cards is over does the lady finally decide to stroll over to the counter to take your order. Slightly irritated by the lack of service, you:

A   Tell her that you had been waiting far too long. You let her you find her attitude disrespectful and that you no longer want a drink. You leave the premises immediately.

B   Ask her if she owns the bar, then proceed to expound your own ideas about customer service and how customers should be treated. The customer should be king and should not have to wait for ten minutes to be waited on, you say, especially when there are no other customers.

C   Quickly realize that you are in Portugal and that you should therefore adapt to the local pace and customs. You completely ignore her bad service, musing about the advantages of a slow pace of life, where people take time to play cards while at work.

Comments

A may reflect your true feelings, but it is best to get used to the fact that service varies greatly in Portugal. It would be best to adopt a more tolerant attitude. B may be valid criticism in your eyes, but it won't get you anywhere in Portugal. People rarely complain, in part because the Portuguese are discreet and don't want to attract attention in public, and in part because they know that a complaint will achieve very little. Since slow service is by no means an exception in Portugal, C is probably your best approach. People working in customer service sometimes overemphasize the social function of their job.

SITUATION TWO

It is one of those rare cold winter days, and a friend offers to drop you off in a small historic town on his way to an evening class and later pick you up at an arranged time. You have been planning an excursion to this little historic town for quite some time and you are grateful that your friend can give you a ride. After an enjoyable afternoon you arrive timely at the specified location and wait by the side of the road for about twenty minutes, before deciding to call him on his cell phone. Your friend is apologetic and tells you that he will pick you up in half an hour. You decide to wait at a nearby café and warm up over a cup of coffee. Half an hour later you are again by the side of the road at the end of town, but your friend is late again. Finally, after waiting in the cold for another twenty minutes, he finally shows up. You enter the car shivering with cold and you ...

- A Thank him for picking you up. You ask him how his class went and then ask him to turn up the heater.
- B Tell him how long you had been waiting, that you are shivering with cold, and that you had hoped to be back at home by this time. Then you ask him, why in the world was he so late?
- C Confront him directly with his negligent attitude. What was he thinking to let you wait in the cold for so long, and then arrive late again?

Comments

A is probably a common solution, since little can be done after the fact. You still get a ride home after all, just a little late. Your best attitude here might be: all's well that ends well.

Although it might be appropriate to let your friend know that you were cold and that you lost your patience, B probably goes a little too far and is a bit too confrontational. C is obviously not the right way to proceed in Portugal. For the Portuguese, friendship is more important than trying to make a point, and open conflict is avoided as much as possible. Time is also a very flexible concept for the Portuguese, and the simple fact that the friend offered you a ride is seen as a favor, regardless of the fact that he picked you up very late.

SITUATION THREE

You have a business in Portugal or you are perhaps a manager at a large international firm in Portugal. An international soccer championship will soon take place, and because of the time difference, most of the games of the Portuguese team will take place during working hours. Some of your employees or perhaps workers' representatives approach you and ask you to allow the workers to watch the games of the Portuguese team on TV at work. Surprised by this request, you ...

A Tell your employees that you expect them to tend to their responsibilities, which is what you hired them for. If workers continually look for excuses to take breaks and time off from work, you might as well close down the business.

B Agree enthusiastically. After all you are a soccer fan yourself, and you are looking forward to watching the games at work together with your employees.

C Tell your employees to show you the exact schedule of the games and come back to discuss the issue in more detail. Perhaps a rotating schedule can be implemented so everyone can watch part of the game, while at the same time the most important work still gets done.

Comments

A would be the most culturally insensitive response. Employees are aware of their rights and duties, but they also expect certain perks from their employers from time to time. This raises morale and promotes productivity and a pleasant work environment. An understanding and generous boss can more easily ask for extra favors from his employees than one who strictly follows rules and policies. B is the answer all soccer fans among the employees would like to hear. However, this may not always be practical for the business. C is the answer that comes closest to a compromise that satisfies both sides. In this case, the most important work will still get done, and employees get a chance to watch part of the game.

SITUATION FOUR

You are at the local telephone office where you waited in line to use one of the computers to check your e-mail. After trying unsuccessfully several times to open the browser software, you address the lady at the counter and tell her that you cannot open the web browser, because the computer displays a sign-in screen that asks for an administrator password. The employee tells you that it is your password that you need to enter. You tell her that the sign-in screen comes up when the computer is first turned on and that it is not your password that is required, but the password of the telephone company to start up the computer.

The employee becomes impatient and insists that it is your password, which she has nothing to do with and can do nothing about. Aware of the employee's ignorance and unhelpfulness, you …

A   Tell her that you have never observed such ignorance, lack of professionalism, and unhelpfulness, and you promise her that you will write about this incident in your book about Portugal.

B   Ask the employee for her name and ask for her supervisor's name and contact information. A condescending attitude paired with ignorance is too much for anyone to handle from a counter person.

C   Quietly go back to your computer station, pack your things and leave the telephone office, after realizing that this is a no-win situation.

Comments

A probably reflects your accurate feelings, but the Portuguese rarely engage in arguments in public. This approach might help you vent your anger, but it is the least recommended solution. The Portuguese do not argue in public over a trifle, so answer A could be called very "un-Portuguese." Again, answer B goes a little too far over an incident that most Portuguese would simply shrug off and regard as a normal occurrence when dealing with customer service personnel. C is doubtlessly the most typical response among the Portuguese, who don't easily complain.

DO'S AND DON'TS APPENDIX

Do's

- Shake hands when greeting someone or when introduced to someone. The Portuguese customarily shake hands with everybody present.
- Use the polite form of speech to address people older than yourself, those whose position demands respect, and people you have just met.
- Men should take their hat off when entering a church, and women should cover their shoulders.
- Open car doors for women, hold doors open for them, and help carry their bags or luggage. Portuguese women are used to men treating them with courtesy and respect and to act as gentlemen. Likewise, elderly people expect to be treated with respect and courtesy.
- On a bus, streetcar, or subway, offer your seat to the elderly and to pregnant women.
- Be patient when waiting for appointments, guests, and so on. The Portuguese customarily arrive late for all but the most important business meetings.
- Give the self-appointed parking attendants some change for looking after your parked car. When taking a taxi, round up the fare.
- Learn a little bit about soccer, Portugal's most popular sport and a national passion. Knowing a few players and teams by name will help break the ice and impress the Portuguese, especially men.
- Be patient when waiting in line. This is an inevitable part of daily life, which the Portuguese accept with nonchalance.
- As a sign of respect, wipe your feet on the doormat before entering someone's home.

Don'ts

- Don't point your finger at people or stare at them. This is impolite.
- Don't eat food with your fingers. Always use a napkin to hold sandwiches and other snacks.
- Don't be alarmed when people stand close to you in public or in conversation. Personal space is not very important to the Portuguese.
- Don't be alarmed when people, especially men, frequently touch your arm or shoulder when talking to you. This is normal behavior during conversation.
- Don't shy away from kisses. In greeting women commonly offer both cheeks to men and women alike for a light kiss.
- Don't curse in public or raise your voice. It is considered a sign of bad manners and low social status.
- Don't use blasphemous language. The Portuguese are a religious people and might be offended.
- Don't make noises while eating. Smacking, slurping, burping, or making noise with plates and cutlery is considered a sign of bad manners.
- Don't use sarcasm and irony in conversation. The Portuguese are a courteous and inoffensive people who take seriously what other people say about them.

GLOSSARY

LIST OF FOOD ITEMS

Meat, Dairy, and Poultry
bife – beefsteak
borrego – young male lamb
cabrito – young goat, kid
carne – meat
chouriço – smoked sausage
coelho – rabbit
cordeiro – lamb
costeleta – chop, cutlet
costela – rib
fiambre – cured cold meat, cold ham
fígado – liver
frios – general term for cold cuts
frango – chicken
leitão – suckling pig
leite – milk
lombo – pork loin
ovo – egg
pato – duck
perdiz – partridge
peru – turkey
porco – pork
presunto – smoked, salted ham
queijo – cheese
requeijão – a type of cottage cheese

salpicão – sausage of pickled pork
salsicha - small sausage, such as hot dog
vitela - veal

Seafood

amêijoas – clams
atum – tuna
bacalhau – dried, salted cod
camarão – shrimp
carapau – horse mackerel
choco – cuttlefish
enguia – eel
gamba – prawn
lagosta – lobster
linguado – sole
lula – squid
mariscos – shellfish
mexilhões – mussels
peixe – fish
peixe espada – swordfish
pescada – whiting, a type of hake
polvo – octopus
robalo – sea bass
santola – crab
sardinha – sardine
sargo – sea bream
truta – trout

Ways of Preparing Food

assado – roasted, baked
cozido – boiled
empada – pastry filled with meat

espetada – a variety of meats or fish grilled on skewers
estufado – braised
frito – fried
fumado – smoked
grelhado – grilled
guisado – stewed
recheado – stuffed
refogado – fried in butter or olive oil

Vegetables and Legumes

abóbora – pumpkin, squash
azeitona – olive
alface – lettuce
alho – garlic
brócolos – broccoli
cebola – onion
cenora – carrot
cogumelo – mushroom
couve – kale
couve-flor – cauliflower
ervilha – pea
espinafre – spinach
favas – broad/large beans
feijão – general term for a variety of dried beans
feijão verde – green beans
grão – chickpeas
hortaliça – vegetables, greenery
legumes – vegetables
pepino – cucumber
pimentão – green pepper
salada – salad
tomate – tomato

Starches

arroz – rice
batata – potato
batatas fritas – French fries
pão – bread

Condiments and Spices

aceite – olive oil
canela – cinnamon
caril – curry
cravo – cloves
pimenta preta – black pepper
piripiri – small, red, hot pepper
sal – salt
vinagre – vinegar
alecrim – rosemary
salsa – parsley
coentro – coriander
manjericão – basil

Desserts (Sobremesa)

arroz doce (sweet rice) – a sweet rice pudding with cinnamon
gelado – ice cream
maçã assada – baked apple, a popular dessert
pudim flã – caramel pudding
queijo com compota – fresh cheese (such as *requeijão*) served with a variety of fruit compotes, such as pumpkin; popular in the Beiras region

Fruits (Frutos)

ameixa – plum
amêndoa – almond

amora – blackberry
ananás – pineapple
banana – banana
castanha – chestnut
cereja – cherry
figo – fig
laranja – orange
limão – lemon
maçã – apple
medronho – arbutus berry, the fruit of the strawberry tree
melancia – watermelon
melão – melon
morango – strawberry
noz – nut, usually walnut
pêra – pear
pêssego – peach
uva – grape

CONVERSATION BASICS

The following section provides a basic vocabulary for everyday situations. To be well prepared for the challenges of communicating in Portuguese, it is best to buy a phrase book with a variety of conversation topics, as well as a small dictionary.

Greetings and Basic Phrases

good morning – *bom dia;* the plural form *bons dias* is also used
good afternoon – *boa tarde;* the plural form *boas tardes* is also used
good night – *boa noite*; the plural form *boas noites* is also used
good bye – *adeus; até à vista*
bye bye – *tchau*; (from the Italian *ciao*)
hello – *olá*
Everything's well? – *Tudo bem?*
See you soon; see you later – *até logo*

yes – *sim*

no – *não*

please – *faz favor*

thank you – *obrigado* (when the speaker is male); *obrigada* (when the speaker is female)

How are you? – *Como está? Como vai?*

I am fine, thank you – *Estou bem, muito obrigado/obrigada*

you are welcome – *de nada*

don't mention it – *não há; não tem de que*

never mind – *não tem importância*

I am sorry – *desculpe-me,* or *desculpe*

excuse me – *perdão; com licença* (when passing or stepping ahead of someone)

It doesn't matter – *não faz mal*

Congratulations! – *parabéns!*

Happy birthday! – *Feliz aniversário!*

Have a good trip! – *Boa viagem!*

Good Luck! – *Boa sorte!*

Glad to meet you – *muito prazer; prazer em conhecé-lo*

Do you speak English? – *Fala inglês?*

I don't speak Portuguese – *Não falo português*

Do you understand? – *Compreende?*

I don't understand you – *Não compreendo-o*

I don't know – *Não sei*

Could you speak more slowly? – *Pode falar mais devagar?*

What is your name? – *Como se chama?*

My name is... – *Chamo-me...*

On the Telephone

Hello – *Estou;* common short form: *'tó* ; (literally: 'I am here', or 'It's me')

Is Mary there? – *A Maria está?*

Who is talking? – *Quem fala? Quem está falando?*

I would like to talk to... – *Queria falar com ...*
Who is calling? – *É da parte de quem?*
It is Paul – *É o Paulo*

Getting Around

Where is – Onde é...? Onde está…?
the bathroom/the toilet – *a casa de banho/ o lavabo*
the bus terminal – *o terminal rodoviáro; a central de camionagem*
the railway station – *a estação de caminhos de ferro*
the city center – *o centro da cidade*
the bust stop – *a paragem de autocarros*
the subway – *o metro*
the shopping mall – *o centro comercial*
the post office – *o posto de correios*
Where is the nearest telephone? – *Onde está o telefone mais próximo?*

Where is there...? – *Onde há...?*
a restaurant – *um restaurante*
a hotel – *um hotel*
a grocery store – *uma mercearia*
a bank – *um banco*
to the left – *à esquerda*
to the right – *à direita*
one block – *um quarteirão*
across the street – *ao outro lado da rua*

At what time does the ... open? - *A que horas abre...?*
the newsstand – *o quiosque*
the bookstore – *a livraria*
the tourist office – *o posto de turismo*
the money exchange office – *a casa de câmbio*
What is the exchange rate? – *Qual é a tarifa de câmbio?*
I would like to change money – *Queria trocar dinheiro*

Can you change this bill? – *Pode trocar esta nota?*

When does the bus arrive? – *Quando chega o autocarro?*
Does the bus go to...? – *O autocarro vai para...?*
the beach – *a praia*
the soccer stadium – *o estádio de futébol*
How much is the fare? – *Quanto custa o bilhete?*
Is this taxi free? – *Este táxi está livre?*
I would like to go to the airport – *Quero ir ao aeroporto*
to the city hall – *à Câmara Municipal*

At what time does the ... leave? – *A que hora parte/sai ..*
the airplane – *o avião*
the boat – *o barco*
the bus – *o autocarro*
the excursion – *a excursão*
the train – *o comboio*

Shopping

How much is it? – *Quanto custa? Quanto é isto?*
I would like to buy... – *Queria comprar...*
a pair of pants – *uma calça*
a skirt – *uma saia*
a shirt – *uma camisa*
a t-shirt – *uma camiseta*
My size is... – *Meu tamanho é...*
I would like to try this on – *Queria provar isto*
I like that – *Eu gosto disso*
Is there a discount? – *Tem desconto?*
sale – *saldo*
cheap – *barato*
expensive – *caro*
good – *bom*

Eating and Drinking

I would like... – *Queria...*
a glass of wine – *um copo de vinho*
a sparkling mineral water – *uma água mineral com gas*
Can I see the menu? – *Posso ver a ementa?*
What is the special of the day? – *Qual é o prato do dia?*
May we have the bill, please? – *Pode-nos trazer a conta, faz favor?*
How much do I owe you? – *Quanto lhe devo?*

Emergencies

This is an emergency – *Isto é uma emergência*
I need help – *Preciso de ajuda*
I am lost – *Estou perdido* (masc.)*/perdida* (fem.)
Can you help me? – *Pode ajudar-me?*
Where can I find a doctor? – *Onde posso encontrar um médico ?*
Where is the health center? – *Onde fica o centro de saúde?*
Where is there a doctor who speaks English? – *Onde tem um médico que fala inglês?*

Call ... – *Chame...*
the police – *a polícia*
the fire department – *os bombeiros*
an ambulance – *uma ambulância*
a health clinic – *um posto médico*
the emergency room – *o serviço de urgência*

Where is there a hospital nearby? – *Onde há um hospital por aqui?*
I am sick – *Estou doente*
It hurts here – *Dói-me aqui*
I have a ... – *Tenho uma...*
headache – *dor de cabeça*
stomach ache – *dor de estômago*
sore throat – *dor de garganta*

wound – *uma ferida*
toothache – *dor de dentes*
I have a temperature – *Estou com febre*
I have diarrhea – *Tenho diarréia*
I have a cold – *Estou constipado* (masculine) / *constipada* (feminine)

Time and Date

The most common way of telling the time in Portugal is the 24-hour clock, although the 12-hour clock is also sometimes used. e.g. 10am is *dez horas da manhã* (10 o'clock in the morning) and 4pm is *dezaseis horas* (16 hours) , or less frequently *quatro horas da tarde* (4 o'clock in the afternoon). 11pm is *vinte e três horas* (23 hours), or less frequently *onze horas da noite* (11 o'clock at night). Time is expressed in the plural (except when saying *é uma hora*— it is one o'clock):

São oito horas (it is 8 o'clock; plural),
but: *é meio-dia* (it is noon; singular).
São vinte e uma horas da noite (it is 9pm or 21 hours; plural),
but: *é meia-noite* (it is midnight; singular).

What time is it? – *Que horas são?*
It is 3:15pm *São as quinze horas e um quarto* (It is 15 hours and a quarter hour).
It is 7:30am – *São as sete e meia* (It is 7 and a half).
I t is 10:45pm – *São vinte e duas horas e quarenta e cinco minutos* (it is 22 hours and 45 minutes); or: *São um quarto para as vinte e três horas* (it is a quarter hour before 23 hours).
yesterday – *ontem*
today – *hoje*
tomorrow – *amanhã*
morning – *a manhã*
afternoon – *a tarde*
night – *a noite*

noon – *meio-dia*
midnight – *meia-noite*

Days of the Week

A peculiar detail of Portugal's Christian heritage is the fact that Portugal uses a Christian weekly calendar. Instead of weekdays dedicated to pagan gods (as in English, French, Spanish, etc.), the Portuguese use ordinal numbers to indicate the day of the week. The week starts with Sunday.

Sunday – *domingo* (Day of the Lord)
Monday – *segunda feira* (second day)
Tuesday – *terça feira* (third day)
Wednesday – *quarta feira* (fourth day)
Thursday – *quinta feira* (fifth day)
Friday – *sexta feira* (sixth day)
Saturday – *sábado* (Sabbath)

What day is today? – *Que dia é hoje?*
Today is Thursday, July 25 – *Hoje é quinta feira, vinte e cinco de julho.*
weekend – *o fim de semana*
holiday – *feriado*
Christmas – *Natal*
New Year – *Ano Novo*
Easter – *Páscoa*
Working days (work week) – *dias úteis*

The Months of the Year

January – *Janeiro*
February – *Fevereiro*
March – *Março*
April – *Abril*
May – *Maio*

June – *Junho*
July – *Julho*
August – *Agosto*
September – *Setembro*
October – *Outubro*
November – *Novembro*
December – *Dezembro*

Years are expressed as simple cardinal numbers, e.g. 1998 is *mil novecentos noventa e oito* (one thousand nine hundred and ninety-eight), 2005 is *dois mil e cinco* (two thousand and five), and so on.

CALENDAR OF FESTIVALS

January 1	Ano Novo (New Year's Day)
March/April	Sexta Feira Santa (Good Friday)
April 25	Dia da Liberdade (Liberty Day)
May 1	Dia do Trabalhador (May Day)
May/June	Corpo de Deus (Corpus Christi)
June 10	Dia de Portugal, de Camões e das Comunidades (Portugal Day)
August 15	Assunção da Virgem Santa Maria (St. Mary's Assumption)
October 5	Dia da República (Day of the Republic)
November 1	Dia de Todos os Santos (All Saints' Day)
December 1	Restauração da Independência de Portugal (Independence Day)
December 8	Imaculada Conceição da Virgem Santa Maria (Our Lady of the Immaculate Conception, the main patron saint of Portugal)
December 25	Natal (Christmas Day)

RESOURCE GUIDE

USEFUL ADDRESSES

Portuguese Embassies and Consulates Abroad

USA
Portuguese Embassy
2125 Kalorama Road, NW, Washington DC 20008
Tel: (202) 328 8610; fax: (202) 462 3726

Consulate General
630 Fifth Avenue, Suite #801 New York, NY 10111
Tel: (212) 765 2980 or 246 4580; fax: (212) 262 2143
cgprtny@aol.com

Canada
Portuguese Embassy (Ottawa)
645 Island Park Drive, Ottawa, ON, K1Y 0B8
Tel: (613) 729 0883; fax: (613) 729 4236
http://www.embportugal-ottawa.org;
embportugal@embportugal-ottawa.org

United Kingdom
Portuguese Embassy
11 Belgrave Square, London SW1X 8PP
Tel: (207) 235 5331; fax: (207) 245 1287
http://www.portembassy.gla.ac.uk

Australia
Portuguese Embassy
23 Culgoa Circuit, O'Malley ACT 2606, Canberra
Tel: 6290 1733; fax: 6290 1957
embportcamb@internode.on.net

Foreign Embassies and Consulates in Portugal

USA
US Embassy
Av. das Forças Armadas, Sete Rios, 1600-081 Lisboa
Tel: 21 727 33 00; fax: 21 726 91 09
http://www.american-embassy.pt

Canada
Canadian Embassy
Avenida da Liberdade 196-200, 3rd Floor, 1269-121 Lisbon
Tel: 21 316 46 00; fax: 21 316 46 93
http://www.dfait-maeci.gc.ca/canadaeuropa/portugal;
lsbon-cs@dfait-maeci.gc.ca

United Kingdom
British Embassy
Rua de São Bernardo 33, 1249-082 Lisboa
Tel: 21 392 40 00; fax: 21 392 41 85
http://www.uk-embassy.pt; ppalisbon@fco.gov.uk

Australia
Australian Embassy
Avenida da Liberdade, 200, 2nd Floor, Lisbon 1250-147
Tel: 21 310 15 00; fax: 21 310 15 55
http://www.portugal.embassy.gov.au

Miscellaneous Addresses

The U.S. Commercial Service, Portugal
U.S. Commercial Service (Lisbon)
Part of the U.S. Commerce Department, this service assists American companies in doing business in Portugal. Address is the same as the U.S. embassy in Lisbon.
Tel: 21 770 25 28; fax: 21 726 89 14
http://www.usatrade.gov/website/ForOffices.nsf/(CountryList)/
Portugal?OpenDocument;
lisbon.office.box@mail.doc.gov

U.S. Commercial Service (Porto)
Avenida da Boavista 3523, Room 501, 4100-139 Porto
Tel: 22 618 66 07; fax: 22 618 66 25
oporto.office.box@mail.doc.gov

American Chamber of Commerce in Portugal
A non-profit organization with the purpose of expanding economic and cultural relations between the USA and Portugal.
Rua D. Estefânia, 155-5° Esq., 1000-154 Lisboa
Tel: 21 357 25 61; fax: 21 357 25 80
http://cca.imediata.pt; nop37676@mail.telepac.pt

The British–Portuguese Chamber of Commerce, Lisbon
A non-profit organization promoting trade and business opportunities between Portugal and the UK.
Rua da Estrela 8, 1200-669 Lisbon
Tel: 21 394 20 20; fax: 21 394 20 29
http://www.bpcc.pt; info@bpcc.pt

The British Council, Lisbon
An international British organization specializing in educational

opportunities and cultural relations. There are centers in Coimbra, Cascais, Almada, Lisbon, and Porto, as well as in a few other towns.
Rua Luís Fernandes 1-3, 1249-062 Lisboa
Tel: 21 32 1 45 00; fax: 21 347 61 51
http://www.pt.britishcouncil.org;
lisbon.enquiries@pt.britishcouncil.org

Agência Portuguese para o Investimento (Invest in Portugal)
A newly created agency as part of the Ministry of Economy that promotes investment in Portugal and monitors all foreign direct investment projects.
Praça do Bom Sucesso 127/131, Sala 702, 4150-146 Porto
Tel: 22 605 53 00; fax: 22 605 53 99
http://www.investinportugal.pt; api@apinvest.pt

Serviço de Estrangeira e Fronteiras (Department of Foreigners and Borders)
Rua Conselheiro José Silvestre Ribeiro 4, 1649-007 Lisboa
Tel: 21 711 50 00; fax: 21 714 03 32
http://www.sef.pt; sef@sef.pt
Algarve Office:
Rua Luis de Camões, n°5, 8000-388 Faro
Tel: 28 980 58 22, or 28 98 8 83 00; fax: 28 980 15 66
dir.algarve@sef.pt

ICEP Portugal—Investment, Commerce and Tourism
Government agency on business and tourism (with English section).
Av. 5 de Outubro, n° 101,1050-051 Lisbon
Tel: 21 790 95 00, Toll-free 808 214 214; fax: 21 793 50 28
http://www.icep.pt; icep@icep.pt

ICEP Overseas Offices:
USA
ICEP, 590 5th Ave., 3rd floor, New York, NY 10036-4702
Tel: (212) 354 4610; fax: (212) 575 4737
http://www.portugal.org; mgarcia@portugal.org

Canada
Delegation of ICEP in Toronto, 60 Bloor Street West, Suite 1005,
Toronto, ONTARIO M4W 3B8
Tel: (416) 921 7376 or 921 4925; fax: (416) 921 1353
iceptor@idirect.com

United Kingdom
ICEP, 2nd and 4th floor, 22-25A Sackville Street, London W1X 1DE
Tel: (207) 494 1517; fax (207) 494 1508

Portugal–US Chamber of Commerce
A professional organization committed to promoting business and
economic partnership between Portugal and the USA.
590 Fifth Avenue, New York, NY 10036
Tel: 212 354 4627; fax: 212 575 4737
http://www.portugal-us.com; PortugueseCham@aol.com

Portuguese Chamber—The Portuguese UK Business Network
1st floor, 22/25a Sackville Street, London W1S 3DR, UK
Tel: 207 494 1844; fax: 207 494 1822
http://www.portuguese-chamber.org.uk;
info@portuguese-chamber.org.uk

Social Clubs in Portugal

American Club of Lisbon
Hotel Sheraton Lisboa, R. Latino Coelho 1–Room 105, 1069-025 Lisbon
Tel: 21 352 93 08; fax: 21 352 93 09
americanclub@mail.telepac.pt

British Community Council Lisbon
The council serves the interests and needs of the British community in the Lisbon area and promotes Anglo-Portuguese friendship and understanding.
http://www.bcclisbon.org; info@bcclisbon.org

International Women in Portugal (IWP)
A social organization for expatriate women with the aim of helping newcomers settle in Portugal.
Estoril Office at Rua de Lisboa Nº 1C, Sala 13, 2765-240 Estoril
Tel: 21 468 39 25
http://www.iwponline.org; iwp@clix.pt

The Royal British Club (Lisbon)
An international business and social club serving the business and social needs of its members within Portugal.
Rua de Lisboa, Nº1C, Sala 13, 2765- 240 Estoril
Tel: 21 468 17 12; fax: 21 468 16 74
http://www.royalbritishclub.pt; info@royalbritishclub.pt

USEFUL WEBSITES

Art and Culture

At-Tambur.com—Músicas do Mundo
A site about traditional Portuguese music and dance.
http://www.attambur.com (with English version)

Instituto Português de Museus (Portuguese Institute of Museums)
http://www.ipmuseus.pt (Portuguese only)

Instituto Português do Património Arquitectónico, IPPAR (Portuguese Institute of Architectural Heritage)
http://www.ippar.pt (Portuguese only)

Madredeus
Homepage of Portugal's best known music group (with English version).
http://madredeus.mind.pt/ or http://www.madredeus.net

Ministério de Cultura (Portuguese Ministry of Culture)
A calendar of cultural programs and events all over Portugal.
http://www.min-cultura.pt (Portuguese only)

Portugal Roots Web
Diverse information about Portuguese culture.
http://www3.sympatico.ca/geoles

The Portuguese Culture Web
Interesting tidbits of cultural information about Portugal.
http://www.portcult.com/

Business and Money

Associação Empresarial de Portugal, AEP (Portuguese Business Association)
Provides a wide range of business services for Portuguese and foreign companies (with English version).
Av. da Boavista 2671, 4100–135 Porto
Tel: 22 615 85 00; fax: 22 617 68 40
http://www.aeportugal.pt

Classic 164 Currency Converter
Current exchange rates for 164 different currencies.
http://www.oanda.com/converter/classic

Currency Exchange Rates
http://www.x-rates.com/

European Central Bank
http://www.ecb.int/

Ministério das Finanças (Portuguese Ministry of Finance)
Information about the tax system in Portugal (with English version).
http://www.dgci.min-financas.pt/dgciappl/informacaodgci.nsf/taxsystem?openview

PortugalOffer—Business, Investment and Industry in Portugal
Represents business interests of 500 Portuguese companies abroad.
http://www.portugaloffer.com; financetar@portugaloffer.com

Portugal in Business
New website by ICEP Portugal (see above) to promote Portugal as a location for investment and tourism.
http://www.portugalinbusiness.com

Western Union

Allows you to send money abroad for pickup at worldwide Western Union agents.

http://www.westernunion.com

Education

GoAbroad.com

A comprehensive database for international education and travel.

http://www.goabroad.com or http://www.studyabroaddirectory.com

International Schools Services (ISS)

Provides listings of American and international schools, as well as teacher placement.

http://www.iss.edu

LanguageSchoolsGuide.com

Useful resource for locating international language schools.

http://www.languageschoolsguide.com

WorldWide Classroom

Extensive listing of international schools.

http://www.worldwide.edu/ci/portugal/index.html

WWTeach—International Education, Schools & Living

Provides links, information, and resources for teachers, students, and parents.

http://members.aol.com/wwteach/Teach.htm

Getting Settled in Portugal

CTT Correios (Portuguese Post Office)
http://www.ctt.pt

Direcção-Geral de Viação (Traffic Department)
Information about driver's licenses, vehicle registration, etc. (with English version)
http://www.dgv.pt

Embassy World
A directory of worldwide embassy/consulate locations.
http://www.embassyworld.com

EPN—Euro Property Network
Europe-wide real estate service.
http://www.europropertynet.com

International Real Estate Digest
The Portugal section provides links to real estate agents and relocation services; some links in English.
http://www.ired.com

Loja do Cidadão (Citizen's Store)
A government service center with branches all over Portugal, where citizens can take care of most bureaucratic processes in one visit, such as payment of utility bills, automobile registration, driver's licenses, ID cards, tax payments, social security and health services, as well as legal advice.
Toll-free: 808 24 11 07
http://www.lojadocidadao.pt/homepage (Portuguese only);
lojadocidadao@lojadocidadao.pt

Páginas Amarelas (Portuguese Yellow Pages)
http://www.paginasamarelas.pt (with English version)

Viviun International Property Listings
Real estate for sale in Portugal.
http://www.viviun.com/Real_Estate/Portugal

White Pages Telephone Directory
http://www.118.pt (with English version)

Health

Centers for Disease Control, Traveler's Health Home Page
Provides health information on specific destinations about outbreaks,
diseases, vaccinations, water safety, and links to other related sites.
http://www.cdc.gov/travel

International Travel and Health
Compiled by the World Health Organization, the website provides
information about vaccination requirements, travel risks and
precautions, accidents, and infectious diseases for most countries.
http://www.who.int/ith

U.S. State Department, Consular Affairs Publications
Provides information about visa requirements, health, safety, U.S.
embassies and consulates, and specific country information worldwide.
http://travel.state.gov/travel_pubs.html

Information about Portugal

Country Briefings
Compiled by the Economist Intelligence Unit, with extensive economic

and political data compiled for 60 countries, including Portugal.
http://www.economist.com/countries/Portugal

Library of Congress Country Studies
Provides detailed economic, historical, social, and political information
on 101 countries.
http://lcweb2.loc.gov/frd/cs/cshome.html

National Statistics Institute of Portugal
Current statistical data for Portugal (with English version).
http://www.ine.pt

Portugal Info
Information about Portugal, mainly for tourists.
http://www.portugal-info.net

Portugal inSite
Official Portuguese tourism site by ICEP (with English version).
http://www.portugalinsite.pt

Portugal-links.com
Lists extensive links about Portugal.
http://www.portugal-links.com

Portugal Virtual
Provides useful links and resources for travel in Portugal.
http://www.portugalvirtual.pt

Portuguese Government Web Portal
Information about the Portuguese government, political programs,
activities, organizations, etc. (with English version).
http://www.portugal.gov.pt

The Algarve Home Page
Comprehensive information about the Algarve.
http://www.algarvenet.com

Welcome to Portugal
Another official ICEP website with information on tourism, trade, and investment.
http://www.portugal.org

Internet Café Directories

Cybercafes.com
Contains a database of 4,200 internet cafés in 140 countries.
http://www.cybercafe.com

The Cybercafé Search Engine
An online database with over 6,000 verified listings of cyber cafés, public Internet access points, and kiosks in 170 countries.
http://cybercaptive.com

Living Abroad

EscapeArtist Home Page
An extensive expatriate website providing resources, links, and information about moving abroad and living overseas. Publishes the free monthly *Escape From America* e-magazine.
http://www.escapeartist.com

Expat Exchange
One of the most extensive expatriate sites online, providing a wealth of resources and articles for expatriates worldwide.
http://www.expatexchange.com

Expatriates.com
Provides an extensive resource directory, discussion board, and so on for expatriates.
http://www.expatriates.com

Overseas Digest
Provides resources for living, studying, and working abroad. Also publishes a monthly online newsletter.
http://overseasdigest.com

OverseasJobs.com
Features international job opportunities for professionals, expatriates, and adventure seekers.
http://www.overseasjobs.com

Newspapers, Radio, and TV

Diário de Notícias
http://www.dn.sapo.pt

Expresso
http://www.expresso.pt

Jornal de Notícias
http://www.jnoticias.pt

Kidon Media Link
A worldwide guide to news sources online.
http://www.kidon.com/media-link/index.shtml

KISSFM Algarve
A commercial radio station in the Algarve with 25% English programming.
http://www.portugal-links.com/kissfm/index.htm

O Público
http://www.publico.pt

Portugal Post (The World News Network)
http://www.portugalpost.com

Radiodifusão Portuguesa SA
http://www.rdp.pt

Radio Televisão Portuguesa, RTP
http://www.rtp.pt

The Portugal News, Portugal's Weekend Newspaper in English
http://www.the-news.net/

Visão Magazine
http://www.visaoonline.pt

Travel Safety

Australian Department of Foreign Affairs and Trade
http://www.dfat.gov.au/travel

Canadian Department of Foreign Affairs and International Trade
Provides travel and safety information.
http://www.dfait-maeci.gc.ca/travel/menu-en.asp

United Kingdom, Foreign & Commonwealth Office (Travel)
The British government department responsible for overseas relations
and foreign affairs; basic information for travelers.
http://www.fco.gov.uk/travel

U.S. Bureau of Consular Affairs
Travel safety information and travel warnings on most countries.
http://travel.state.gov

PORTUGUESE LANGUAGE COURSES

The following section provides a list of Portuguese language schools
in several Portuguese cities. Lisbon and Porto have the largest
selection of language schools. Several international language schools
also have branches in Portugal. Request detailed information before
making a final decision, since prices and quality of courses vary. You
can also find language schools in the Yellow Pages (*Páginas Amarelas*)
under *Escolas de Línguas*.

Berlitz Language School
Av. Conde Valbom, 6-4 Andar, 1050 Lisboa
Tel 21 352 01 23; fax: 21 352 03 02
http://languagecenter.berlitz.com/Lisbon

Cambridge Language School
There are four branches in Lisbon, and one each in Porto, Coimbra,
Almada, and Funchal.
Lisbon address: Av. da Liberdade, 173, 1250-141 Lisboa
Tel: 21 312 46 00; fax: 21 353 47 29
http://www.cambridge.pt; info@cambridge.pt

Centro Europeu de Línguas
Branches in Lisbon and Porto.

Avenida Padre Manuel da Nóbrega, 3A, 1000-222 Lisboa
Tel: 21 840 74 25; fax: 21 848 79 15
http://www.cel.pt; infocel@cel.pt

CIAL–Centro de Línguas

Schools in Lisbon and Faro.
Av. da República, 41-8° Esq., 1050–187 Lisboa
Tel: 21 794 04 48; fax: 21 796 07 83
http://www.cial.pt; portuguese@cial.pt

Inlíngua Porto

Rua Sá da Bandeira, 605 1°Esq., 4000–437 Porto
Tel: 22 339 44 00; fax 22 339 44 09
http://www.inlinguaporto.com; inlingua@mail.telepac.pt

Instituto Português de Línguas

Rua da Misericórdia n° 76 2° Sala 213, 1200–273 Lisboa
Tel: 21 343 18 88 or 21 321 02 96; fax: 21 343 18 88
http://www.iplinguas.pt; iplinguas@mail.telepac.pt

International House

Offers Portuguese classes in nine Portuguese cities, among them
Lisbon, Porto, and Coimbra.
Lisbon address: Rua Marquês Sá da Bandeira, 16, 1050-148 Lisboa
Tel: 21 315 14 96; fax: 21 353 00 81
http://www.international-house.com; info@ihlisbon.com

Línguas e Línguas

Praça Luís Camões, 22-2°dto, 1200–243 Lisboa
Tel: 21 342 96 56; fax: 21 342 96 73
http://www.languagelisboa.net; amlino@iol.pt

Oxford School—Institutos de Línguas

Two schools in Lisbon, one in Cacém.

Rua D. Estefânia, 165-1ƒ,1000-154 Lisboa

Tel: 21 354 65 86; fax: 21 314 11 52

http://www.oxford-school.pt; oxford@mail.telepac.pt

INTERNATIONAL SCHOOLS

If you bring children with you to Portugal, you have to decide whether you should send them to a private school with instruction in English or a public school taught in Portuguese. Younger children generally adapt more easily to a different language of instruction than those who already have attended an English-speaking school for several years.

Most international schools are in Portugal's largest cities Lisbon and Porto, as well as in the Algarve. If there is no international school with instruction in English where you are living, you may decide to send your children to a local public or private school and arrange for English tutoring on the side. You may even consider tutoring your children in English yourself, as a last resort. Since prices vary from school to school and according to the student's age, it is a good idea to contact several schools in your area to find out about prices and compare services. Below I have listed a small number of international schools.

Frank C. Carlucci American International School Lisbon

International co-ed day school, for early childhood through grade 12. U.S. public school curriculum, with other programs like the International Baccalaureate available.

Rua António dos Reis 95, Linhó, 2710–301 Sintra

Tel: 21 923 98 00; fax: 21 923 98 99

http://www.caislisbon.com; info@caislisbon.com

Oporto British School

For students aged four to 18.
Rua da Cerca, 326, 4150-201 Porto
Tel: 22 616 66 60
http://www.oportobritishschool.com; obs.school@mail.telepac.pt

Queen Elizabeth's School

For pre-schoolers till children aged 10.
Rua Filipe Magalhães n°1, 1700–194 Lisbon
Tel: 21 841 01 40; fax: 21 841 01 49
http://www.qes.pt; info@qes.pt

St. Julian's School

For children aged three to 18.
Quinta Nova, 2776–601 Carcavelos
Tel: 21 458 53 00; fax: 21 458 53 13
http://www.stjulians.com; mail@stjulians.com

The International School of the Algarve

For students aged four to 18.
Apartado 80, 8400–400 Lagoa, Algarve
Tel: 28 234 25 47; fax: 28 235 37 87
http://www.internationalschoolofthealgarve.com;
geral@eialgarve.com

FURTHER READING

ART AND CULTURE

Kaplan, Marion. *The Portuguese: The Land and Its People*. Penguin Books, 1998.
A lively and compelling introduction to Portuguese history, culture and life.

Levenson, Jay (ed.). *The Age of the Baroque in Portugal*. Yale University Press, 1993.
A survey of the 18th century Portuguese Baroque period, known for its opulent use of gold.

Sabo, Rioletta, et al. *Portuguese Decorative Tiles: Azulejos*. Abbeville Press Inc., 1998.
A history of the technique and art of Portuguese tile-making.

Serra, João B. (ed.). *Modern Art in Portugal: 1910-1940: The Artist Contemporaries of Fernando Pessoa.* Edition Stemmle, 1998.
An introduction to Portuguese Modernism in painting and sculpture.

Vernon, Paul. *History of the Portuguese Fado*. Ashgate Publishing Company, 1999.
An investigation of the history of Portugal's fado, its music, lyrics, and dissemination. Includes a music CD.

FOOD AND DRINK

Anderson, Jean. *The Food of Portugal*. William Morrow & Co, 1994.
An in-depth introduction to Portuguese cooking with 165 recipes, as well as a wine list and bilingual glossary.

Mayson, Richard, and Johnson, Hugh. *Portugal's Wines & Wine Makers*. Wine Appreciation Guild, 1998.
A review of Portuguese wines, including fortified wines such as Madeira and port.

Mayson, Richard. *Port and the Douro*. Faber & Faber, 2000.
A descriptive history of port wine and the Douro Valley.

Michelin Red Guide 2003 Portugal. Michelin Travel Publications, 2003.
A comprehensive guide to fine dining in Portugal.

Scott-Aiken, Lynelle, and De Vitorino, Clara. *Lonely Planet World Food Portugal*. Lonely Planet, 2002.
A useful guide to food and drink in Portugal.

HISTORY AND POLITICS

Anderson, James M. *The History of Portugal (The Greenwood Histories of the Modern Nations)*. Greenwood Publishing Group, 2000.

Boxer, C.R. *Four Centuries of Portuguese Expansion 1415-1825, A Succinct Survey*. University of California Press, 1969.
A short overview of Portugal's empire during its expansion phase.

Martins, Joaquim P. Oliveira. *The Golden Age of Prince Henry the Navigator*. Simon Publications, 2001.
A biography of the 15th century founder of the Portuguese maritime empire, first published in 1914.

Robertson, Ian C. *The Traveler's History of Portugal*. Interlink Publishing Group, 2002.
Russell-Wood, A.J.R. *A World on the Move: The Portuguese in Africa, Asia, and America, 1415-1808*. Palgrave Macmillan, 1993.
A history of the Portuguese colonial empire.

Saraiva, José Hermano. *Portugal: A Companion History*. Carcanet Press, 1998.

Syrett, Stephen (ed.). *Contemporary Portugal: Dimensions of Economic and Political Change*. Ashgate Publishing Company, 2002.
An overview of Portugal's political and economic life from the 1974 revolution to the present.

LANGUAGE LEARNING

De Vitorino, Clara. *Lonely Planet Portuguese Phrasebook*. Lonely Planet Publications, 2000.
A useful phrasebook of European Portuguese. The book includes a two-way dictionary.

Lathrop, Thomas, et al. *Portugal: Língua e Cultura*. Linguatext Ltd, 1995.
A well-structured textbook for beginner students of European Portuguese.

Nitti, John J., and Ferreira, Michael J. *501 Portuguese Verbs: Fully Conjugated in All the Tenses in a New Easy-to-Learn Format Alphabetically Arranged*. Barron's Educational Series, 1995.

Tyson-Ward, Sue. *Teach Yourself Portuguese Language, Life, and Culture*. McGraw-Hill, 2002.
A do-it-yourself introduction to the Portuguese language, based on relevant cultural topics.

VocabuLearn: Portuguese, Level 1. Penton Overseas, 1998.
Audio book with three hours of instruction.

LITERATURE

The following list of novels is only a small selection of Portugal's large literary production. All the titles listed are either available in English or were at one time translated.

José Saramago

All the Names. Harvest Books, 2001.
Baltasar and Blimunda. Harvest Books, 1998.
Blindness. Harvest Books, 1999.
The Cave. Harvest, 2003.
The Gospel According to Jesus Christ. Harvest Books, 1994.
The History of the Siege of Lisbon. Harvest Books, 1998.
The Stone Raft. Harvest Books, 1996.
The Year of the Death of Ricardo Reis. Harvest Books, 1992.

Miguel Torga

Tales from the Mountain. Q E D Press, 1991.

António Lobo Antunes

Act of the Damned. Grove Press, 1996.
Fado Alexandrino. Grove Press, 1996.
The Inquisitors' Manual. Grove Press, 2002.
The Natural Order of Things. Grove Press 2001.
The Return of the Caravels. Grove Press; 2001.

POETRY

De Amigo, Cantigas. *Songs of a Friend: Love Lyrics of Medieval Portugal: Selections from Cantigas de Amigo*. University of North Carolina Press, 1995.
Translation of a number of medieval love songs from Portugal.

De Camões, Luis. *The Lusiads (Oxford World's Classics)*. Oxford University Press, 2002.
The cornerstone of classical Portuguese literature, this epic poem tells the story of Vasco da Gama's voyage to India in 1498.

Honig, Edwin, and Brown, Susan M. (eds.). *Poems of Fernando Pessoa*. City Lights Books, 1998.
Translation of a number of poems by Fernando Pessoa, including some written under his pseudonyms.

Pessoa, Fernando, and Zenith, Richard (ed.). *The Book of Disquiet*. Penguin, 2002.
A collection of poetry written under Pessoa's pseudonym, Bernardo Soares.

Zenith, Richard (ed.). *Fernando Pessoa & Co: Selected Poems*. Grove Press, 1999.
A selection of Pessoa's major poetry.

TRAVEL GUIDES

Barrett, Pam. *Insight Guide Portugal*. Langenscheidt Publishers, 2000.
Informative illustrated guide to Portuguese history, regions, culture, art, food, and customs.

Davies, Bethan, and Cole, Ben. *Walking in Portugal*. Pili Pala Press, 2000.
Description of 33 walks and hikes in Portugal.

Fisher, John, and Ellingham, Mark. *Portugal: The Rough Guide (9th edition)*. Rough Guides Publications, 2000.
Up-to-date, practical, and comprehensive guide to Portugal.
Fodor's Portugal: The Guide For All Budgets, Where To Stay, Eat, And Explore On And Off The Beaten Path. Fodor's Travel

Publications, 2003.
In-depth guide to Portugal, its regions, and cultural sights.

Prince, Danforth, and Porter, Darwin. *Frommer's Portugal (17th edition)*. John Wiley & Sons, 2002.
Informative guide to Portugal's sights, culture, and vacation destinations.

Symington, Martin. *DK Eyewitness Travel Guide: Portugal: With Madeira and the Azores*. DK Publishing, 2003.
A lavishly illustrated country guide providing essential travel information for visitors to Portugal.

Wilkinson, Julia, and King, John. *Lonely Planet Portugal*. Lonely Planet Publications, 2003, 4th edition.
A popular guide to Portugal for budget travelers.

TRAVEL NARRATIVE

MacAulay, Rose, and Taylor, L.C. (eds.). *They Went to Portugal, Too*. Carcanet Press, 1990.
This book describes the experiences of foreign travelers in Portugal, from the middle ages to the 19th century.

Proper, Datus C. *The Last Old Place: A Search through Portugal*. Simon and Schuster, 1993.
An entertaining travelogue with a lot of cultural insights on Portugal.

Saramago, José. *Journey to Portugal: In Pursuit of Portugal's History and Culture*. Harcourt, 2002.
This honest and satirical travelogue provides an insider's view of Portugal in the early 1980s.

ABOUT THE AUTHOR

Volker Poelzl is an Austrian-born freelance writer, photographer, and world traveler who lives in the USA. He studied Portuguese in Portugal and Brazil and lived in Brazil for several years. He is the author of *Culture Shock! Brazil,* and his interest in the roots of Brazilian culture awakened his curiosity in Portugal. While he found little in Portugal that reminded him of Brazil, he got to know a country with a fascinating culture and a friendly people. Volker lived in Lisbon and extensively explored almost every alley, stairway, and hidden corner of Portugal.

INDEX

Afonso I 20, 59, 65
alcohol 99, 101, 108–112, 152
    port wine 7, 31, 109–111
architecture 43–44, 136–40
art 135–41
    azulejos 140–41

banking 157, 179–80
    credit cards 179–80

cities:
    Aveiro 3, 31
    Braga 3, 5, 31, 136, 146, 151
    Coimbra 3, 8, 116, 119, 124,
    136, 146, 151, 153, 170, 194
    Faro 3
    Lisbon 3, 9, 24, 31, 32, 43, 47,
    119, 123–24, 136–37, 139–40,
    146, 151, 154–55, 163, 165,
    170–71, 183, 194, 196
    Porto 3, 6, 19, 31, 43, 104,
    124, 136, 139–40, 146, 151,
    155, 163, 165, 171, 183, 194
    Setúbal 3, 31, 123
childcare 42
children 44, 52, 56, 169–70
climate 15–16
crime 188, 203
customs 159

da Gama, Vasco 23
dance 120–1
de Camões, Luis 22, 129

despachantes 204–5
divorce 52
domestic help 166
dress 86, 89–90, 208–9
drinks 87–88, 98–99, 112, 151
driving 161, 163, 185–87

economy 30, 31, 42, 200–2
education 38, 193–94, 202
    university 38, 153, 155, 193–94
elderly people 56
electrical equipment 157, 166
emigration 40, 41, 52
employee benefits 197, 198
employment 36, 39–41, 52, 160,
    196–97
Estado Novo 28–29, 35, 40, 118
etiquette, business 205–8
etiquette, social 79–92, 94–96,
    100

family 51–53
festivals 16, 57, 69, 71, 74–77,
    119, 121–27, 153
film 142–43, 155
food 4, 86–88, 97–107
    bacalhau 102–103, 107
foreign exchange 178–80
foreigners:
    immigrants 39–40, 64, 170,
    196
    residents 3–4, 170–71, 196
    workers

gender issues 36–39, 52

healthcare 190–91
  hospitals 191–92
housing 43, 163–65
hygiene 189

labor unions 203
language 210–19

marriage 52, 55, 68–69
mass media 181–82
minorities 4
museum 139–40, 155
music 116–8, 132–35
  fado 50, 60–61, 117–19, 151

nightlife 151–52

parks 15, 146
passports 157–58, 162
performing arts groups 154
Pessoa, Fernando 60, 130, 150
pets 159–60
police 187
political parties 33
population 2, 3, 36
postal service 174–75, 180
poverty 35, 36
Prince Henry the Navigator 11, 21
public transportation 163, 182–84

race relations 39, 40
regions:
  Alentejo 9, 16, 47, 104–5, 108,
    115, 123–24, 136
  Algarve 4, 10–11, 20, 123,
    146–47, 152, 196
  Azores 11, 16, 21, 123, 159

Beiras 4, 7, 13, 15, 18, 104–5,
    108, 125–26
  Douro 6, 108–9, 124, 126
  Estremadura 8–9, 108, 123,
    125, 147
  Madeira Islands 11–12, 21,
    127, 159
  Minho 4–5, 108, 115, 123–26,
  Ribatejo 8–9, 108, 125, 127
  Trás-os-Montes 6, 13, 15, 104,
    115
religion 61, 65–68, 70–74, 95–96
rental contracts 165
residency permit 160
revolution 29, 35, 48, 66, 118,
    131, 193, 201–2

Salazar, António 28–29, 35, 40,
    201
Saramago, José 48, 50, 131
saudade 58–59
shopping 172–74
Spanish rule 23–24, 49, 59, 129
sports 147–48
  soccer 61–62, 146–47
superstitions 78, 85

taxes 160–61, 180, 195, 198
telecommunications 175–78
time 16
topography 2

utilities 165–66

vaccinations 159, 189
Vicente, Gil 129, 154
visas 160, 196

wages 36, 38, 166, 196–97